Driving Theory
Test
2000/2001
Questions

Driving Theory
Test
2000/2001
Questions

Including questions and answers valid for
tests taken from 4th September 2000.

Published by BSM
in association with
Virgin Publishing

First published in the UK in 2000 by
The British School of Motoring Ltd
1 Forest Road
Feltham
Middlesex
TW13 7RR

Copyright © 2000 The British School of Motoring Ltd

1st reprint 2001

ISBN 0 7535 0560 6

Cover picture and cartoons by Marc Lacey

Design, typesetting and reprographics by Prima Creative Services

Printed in Italy

Contents

DRIVING THEORY TEST QUESTIONS

Foreword

Driving is an enjoyable and valuable life skill which is why every year nearly a million new learner drivers take to the road, each one of them with one clear aim. This aim is almost certainly the same as yours – to gain their full driving licence.

There is no substitute for practical experience when learning to drive. The best way to gain this is by taking lessons with a good professional driving instructor who uses the most up-to-date teaching techniques in a modern, dual-controlled car. However, it has always been equally important to prepare for your driving lessons and, since the introduction of the Theory Test, this is doubly true.

Driving Theory Test Questions contains the revised set (valid from 4th September 2000) of official Driving Standards Agency questions which are currently published and which may be included in the actual examination.

This book is an ideal study aid which allows you to test and revise your knowledge. It has been designed for use in conjunction with its companion volumes, *Pass Your Driving Theory Test and Pass Your Driving Test.*

Driving Theory Test Questions allows you to check your level of knowledge by presenting you with real examination questions. The questions are set out under topic headings, and as you work through each section you will prove to yourself that you not only understand what you have learnt, but can demonstrate this by answering the question correctly.

In doing so, you will gradually boost your confidence and thereby recognise when you are ready to take and pass your Theory Test.

Your driving instructor will help you to plan your studies and ensure that you fully understand why the knowledge you acquire is essential to keep you safe on

the road, as well as to take you past that first all important hurdle of passing your Theory Test.

There are no short cuts to becoming a safe and competent motorist, but that does not mean that you cannot enjoy yourself while learning.

Driving Theory Test Questions and its companion volumes, will, I hope, bring the Theory Test alive and make it relevant, and at the same time it should also help you develop your driving skills.

In 90 years of teaching people to drive, BSM instructors have helped millions of people pass their driving test.

In my view, Driving Theory Test Questions completes the best set of books available to help you make the most of your driving lessons and ensure that you prepare for both the theory and practical parts of your driving test in a structured and positive way.

Keith Cameron
Road Safety Adviser

Keith Cameron is one of Britain's leading authorities on motoring and driver education. He has held a number of senior positions within the Department of Transport, including Chief Driving Examiner where he had responsibility for all UK driving tests.

Introduction

The driving test was first introduced to the UK back in 1935. Since that time millions of people have passed the driving test and gained their motoring freedom, many taught by BSM instructors.

In 1996 a separate theory test was introduced in order to test driving knowledge and attitude. This theory test must be passed before a learner driver can apply for a practical driving test. In January 2000 the theory test was computerised. During your test, questions will appear on a computer screen. You select your answers by simply touching the screen. This 'touch screen' system has been carefully designed to make it easy to use.

BSM centres all have touch screen PCs to test your theory knowledge and allow you to practise using the same technology as you'll find in the actual theory exam. Called Theory Online, access to the BSM computers is available free to anyone taking driving lessons with BSM instructors. For details of your nearest BSM centre please call 08457 276 276.

Driving Theory Test Questions contains the official Driving Standards Agency questions which are currently published and which may be included in the actual examination. That means there are a lot of questions in this book (over 1,000), but when you take your Theory Test, you won't be expected to answer all of them! The Test will only have 35 questions for you to answer.

I am sure your main aim is to pass the Theory Test. Nevertheless, I strongly urge to do more than simply attempt to learn the answers parrot fashion. Not only will you find such a method of learning very tedious, you will also miss out on the chance to understand the significance of the information you are learning and make use of it when you practise with your instructor.

Plus don't forget to use the BSM Theory online computers to give you the best chance of passing first time.

Driving Theory
Test
Questions
2000/2001

Alertness

BSM
We won't fail you

Question 1

Before you make a U-turn in the road, you should

Mark one answer

[a] give an arm signal as well as using your indicators

[b] signal so that other drivers can slow down for you

[c] look over your shoulder for a final check

[d] select a higher gear than normal

Question 2

To move off safely from a parked position you should

Mark one answer

[a] signal if other drivers will need to slow down

[b] leave your motorcycle on its stand until the road is clear

[c] give an arm signal as well as using your indicators

[d] look over your shoulder for a final check

Question 3

As a driver what does the term 'Blind Spot' mean?

Mark one answer

[a] An area covered by your right hand mirror

[b] An area not covered by your headlights

[c] An area covered by your left hand mirror

[d] An area not seen in your mirrors

Question 4

Objects hanging from your interior mirror may

Mark two answers

[a] restrict your view

[b] improve your driving

[c] distract your attention

[d] help your concentration

Question 5

You are most likely to lose concentration when driving if you

Mark two answers

[a] use a mobile phone

[b] listen to very loud music

[c] switch on the heated rear window

[d] look at the door mirrors

Question 6

Which FOUR are most likely to cause you to lose concentration while you are driving?

Mark four answers

[a] Using a mobile phone

[b] Talking into a microphone

[c] Tuning your car radio

[d] Looking at a map

[e] Checking the mirrors

[f] Using the demisters

Question 7

When riding, your shoulders obstruct the view in your mirrors. To overcome this you should

Mark one answer

- ⓐ indicate earlier than normal
- ⓑ fit smaller mirrors
- ⓒ extend the mirror arms
- ⓓ brake earlier than normal

Question 8

You want to change lanes in busy, moving traffic. Why could looking over your shoulder help?

Mark two answers

- ⓐ Mirrors may not cover blind spots
- ⓑ To avoid having to give a signal
- ⓒ So traffic ahead will make room for you
- ⓓ So your balance will not be affected
- ⓔ Following motorists would be warned

Question 9

You are about to turn right. What should you do just before you turn?

Mark one answer

- ⓐ Give the correct signal
- ⓑ Take a 'lifesaver' glance over your shoulder
- ⓒ Select the correct gear
- ⓓ Get in position ready for the turn

Question 10

What is the 'lifesaver' when riding a motorcycle?

Mark one answer

- ⓐ A certificate every motorcyclist must have
- ⓑ A final, rearward glance before changing direction
- ⓒ A part of the motorcycle tool kit
- ⓓ A mirror fitted to check blind spots

Question 11

You are driving on a wet road. You have to stop your vehicle in an emergency. You should

Mark one answer

- ⓐ apply the handbrake and footbrake together
- ⓑ keep both hands on the wheel
- ⓒ select reverse gear
- ⓓ give an arm signal

Question 12

You see road signs showing a sharp bend ahead. What should you do?

Mark one answer

- ⓐ Continue at the same speed
- ⓑ Slow down as you go around the bend
- ⓒ Slow down as you come out of the bend
- ⓓ Slow down before the bend

Question 13

As you approach this bridge you should

Oncoming vehicles in middle of road

Mark three answers

ⓐ move into the middle of the road to get a better view

ⓑ slow down

ⓒ get over the bridge as quickly as possible

ⓓ consider using your horn

ⓔ find another route

ⓕ beware of pedestrians

Question 14

When following a large vehicle you should keep well back because

Mark one answer

ⓐ it allows you to corner more quickly

ⓑ it helps the large vehicle to stop more easily

ⓒ it allows the driver to see you in the mirrors

ⓓ it helps you to keep out of the wind

Question 15

In which of these situations should you avoid overtaking?

Mark one answer

ⓐ Just after a bend

ⓑ In a one-way street

ⓒ On a 30 mph road

ⓓ Approaching a dip in the road

Question 16

Which of the following may cause loss of concentration on a long journey?

Mark four answers

ⓐ Loud music

ⓑ Arguing with a passenger

ⓒ Using a mobile phone

ⓓ Putting in a cassette tape

ⓔ Stopping regularly to rest

ⓕ Pulling up to tune the radio

Question 17

You should not use a mobile phone whilst driving

Mark one answer

ⓐ until you are satisfied that no other traffic is near

ⓑ unless you are able to drive one handed

ⓒ because it might distract your attention from the road ahead

ⓓ because reception is poor when the engine is running

Question 18

Your vehicle is fitted with a hands free phone system. Using this equipment whilst driving

Mark one answer

[a] is quite safe as long as you slow down

[b] could distract your attention from the road

[c] is recommended by *The Highway Code*

[d] could be very good for road safety

Question 19

Using a hands-free phone is likely to

Mark one answer

[a] improve your safety

[b] increase your concentration

[c] reduce your view

[d] divert your attention

Question 20

Using a mobile phone while you are driving

Mark one answer

[a] is acceptable in a vehicle with power steering

[b] will reduce your field of vision

[c] could distract your attention from the road

[d] will affect your vehicle's electronic systems

Question 21

This road marking warns

Mark one answer

[a] drivers to use the hard shoulder

[b] overtaking drivers there is a bend to the left

[c] overtaking drivers to move back to the left

[d] drivers that it is safe to overtake

Question 22

You are travelling along this narrow country road. When passing the cyclist you should go

Mark one answer

[a] slowly, sounding the horn as you pass

[b] quickly, leaving plenty of room

[c] slowly, leaving plenty of room

[d] quickly, sounding the horn as you pass

Question 23

Your vehicle is fitted with a hand-held telephone. To use the telephone you should

Mark one answer

ⓐ reduce your speed
ⓑ find a safe place to stop
ⓒ steer the vehicle with one hand
ⓓ be particularly careful at junctions

Question 24

Your mobile phone rings while you are on the motorway. Before answering you should

Mark one answer

ⓐ reduce your speed to 50 mph
ⓑ pull up on the hard shoulder
ⓒ move into the left hand lane
ⓓ stop in a safe place

Question 25

To answer a call on your mobile phone while travelling you should

Mark one answer

ⓐ reduce your speed wherever you are
ⓑ stop in a proper and convenient place
ⓒ keep the call time to a minimum
ⓓ slow down and allow others to overtake

Question 26

Your mobile phone rings while you are travelling. You should

Mark one answer

ⓐ stop immediately
ⓑ answer it immediately
ⓒ pull up in a suitable place
ⓓ pull up at the nearest kerb

Question 27

You should ONLY use a mobile phone when

Mark one answer

ⓐ receiving a call
ⓑ suitably parked
ⓒ driving at less than 30 mph
ⓓ driving an automatic vehicle

Question 28

What is the safest way to use a mobile phone in your vehicle?

Mark one answer

ⓐ Use hands free equipment
ⓑ Find a suitable place to stop
ⓒ Drive slowly on a quiet road
ⓓ Direct your call through the operator

Question 29

You are riding at night. You have your headlight on main beam. Another vehicle is overtaking you. When should you dip your headlight?

Mark one answer

- ⓐ When the other vehicle signals to overtake
- ⓑ As soon as the other vehicle moves out to overtake
- ⓒ As soon as the other vehicle passes you
- ⓓ After the other vehicle pulls in front of you

Question 30

On a motorcycle you should only use a mobile telephone when you

Mark one answer

- ⓐ have a pillion passenger to help
- ⓑ have parked in a safe place
- ⓒ have a motorcycle with automatic gears
- ⓓ are travelling on a quiet road

Question 31

On a long motorway journey boredom can cause you to feel sleepy.
You should

Mark two answers

- ⓐ leave the motorway and find a safe place to stop
- ⓑ keep looking around at the surrounding landscape
- ⓒ drive faster to complete your journey sooner
- ⓓ ensure a supply of fresh air into your vehicle
- ⓔ stop on the hard shoulder for a rest

Question 32

You are riding at night and are dazzled by the headlights of an oncoming car.
You should

Mark one answer

- ⓐ slow down or stop
- ⓑ close your eyes
- ⓒ flash your headlight
- ⓓ turn your head away

Question 33

You are driving at dusk. You should switch your lights on

Mark two answers

(a) even when street lights are not lit

(b) so others can see you

(c) only when others have done so

(d) only when street lights are lit

Question 34

Why are these yellow lines painted across the road?

Mark one answer

(a) To help you choose the correct lane

(b) To help you keep the correct separation distance

(c) To make you aware of your speed

(d) To tell you the distance to the roundabout

Question 35

You are riding along a motorway. You see an accident on the other side of the road. Your lane is clear. You should

Mark one answer

(a) assist the emergency services

(b) stop, and cross the road to help

(c) concentrate on what is happening ahead

(d) place a warning triangle in the road

Question 36

Which of the following should you do before stopping your vehicle?

Mark one answer

(a) Sound the horn

(b) Use the mirrors

(c) Select a higher gear

(d) Flash your headlights

Question 37

You are approaching traffic lights that have been on green for some time. You should

Mark one answer

(a) accelerate hard

(b) maintain your speed

(c) be ready to stop

(d) brake hard

Question 38

In motorcycling, the term 'lifesaver' refers to

Mark one answer

ⓐ a final rearward glance

ⓑ an approved safety helmet

ⓒ a reflective jacket

ⓓ the two-second rule

Question 39

Riding a motorcycle when you are cold could cause you to

Mark one answer

ⓐ be more alert

ⓑ be more relaxed

ⓒ react more quickly

ⓓ lose concentration

Question 40

You are riding at night and are dazzled by the lights of an approaching vehicle. What should you do?

Mark one answer

ⓐ Switch off your headlight

ⓑ Switch to main beam

ⓒ Slow down and stop

ⓓ Flash your headlight

Question 41

When you are moving off from behind a parked car you should

Mark three answers

ⓐ look round before you move off

ⓑ use all the mirrors on the vehicle

ⓒ look round after moving off

ⓓ use the exterior mirrors only

ⓔ give a signal if necessary

ⓕ give a signal after moving off

Answers and explanations

Q001 c You should always check your blind spot just before moving off or starting a manoeuvre.

Q002 d

Q003 d

Q004 a,c

Q005 a,b

Q006 a,b,c,d

Q007 c Mirrors should be adjusted to give you the best view of the road behind. If your shoulders or elbows obstruct the view behind you should fit alternative mirrors with longer stems.

Q008 a,e

Q009 b

Q010 b

Q011 b This helps you maintain control of your car.

Q012 d

Q013 b,d,f

Q014 c

Q015 d You cannot see if a vehicle coming towards you is hidden by the dip.

Q016 a,b,c,d

Q017 c

Q018 b

Q019 d You are not allowed to use a hand-held mobile phone whilst driving. Even a hands-free system can distract your attention from the road.

Q020 c

Q021 c

Q022 c

Q023 b You must not use a hand-held telephone while you are driving.

Q024 d If it's a hand-held phone you must pull up before answering. If it's hands-free it is still advisable to stop.

Q025 b

Q026 c Answering a mobile phone whilst driving might distract your attention. You should pull up first.

Q027 b

Q028 b

Answers and explanations

Q029 c

Q030 b Using a mobile phone can distract your attention from the road ahead.

Q031 a,d

Q032 a

Q033 a,b

Q034 c

Q035 c

Q036 b

Q037 c

Q038 a

Q039 d

Q040 c

Q041 a,b,e

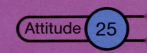

Driving Theory
Test
Questions
2000/2001

Attitude

Question 1

A pelican crossing that crosses the road in a STRAIGHT line and has a central island MUST be treated as

Mark one answer

- ⓐ one crossing in daylight only
- ⓑ one complete crossing
- ⓒ two separate crossings
- ⓓ two crossings during darkness

Question 2

You are approaching a pelican crossing. The amber light is flashing. You must

Mark one answer

- ⓐ give way to pedestrians who are crossing
- ⓑ encourage pedestrians to cross
- ⓒ not move until the green light appears
- ⓓ stop even if the crossing is clear

Question 3

You are approaching a zebra crossing. Pedestrians are waiting to cross. You should

Mark one answer

- ⓐ give way to the elderly and infirm only
- ⓑ slow down and prepare to stop
- ⓒ use your headlights to indicate they can cross
- ⓓ wave at them to cross the road

Question 4

You are riding towards a zebra crossing. Pedestrians are waiting to cross. You should

Mark one answer

- ⓐ give way to the elderly and infirm only
- ⓑ slow down and prepare to stop
- ⓒ use your headlights to indicate they can cross
- ⓓ wave at them to cross the road

Question 5

At puffin crossings which light will not show to a driver?

Mark one answer

- ⓐ Flashing amber
- ⓑ Red
- ⓒ Steady amber
- ⓓ Green

Question 6

You are approaching a red light at a puffin crossing. Pedestrians are on the crossing. The red light will stay on until

Mark one answer

- ⓐ you start to edge forward on to the crossing
- ⓑ the pedestrians have reached a safe position
- ⓒ the pedestrians are clear of the front of your vehicle
- ⓓ a driver from the opposite direction reaches the crossing

Question 7

You could use the 'Two-Second Rule'

Mark one answer

[a] before restarting the engine after it has stalled

[b] to keep a safe gap from the vehicle in front

[c] before using the 'Mirror-Signal-Manoeuvre' routine

[d] when emerging on wet roads

Question 8

A two-second gap between yourself and the car in front is sufficient when conditions are

Mark one answer

[a] wet

[b] good

[c] damp

[d] foggy

Question 9

'Tailgating' means

Mark one answer

[a] using the rear door of a hatchback car

[b] reversing into a parking space

[c] following another vehicle too closely

[d] driving with rear fog lights on

Question 10

You are driving on a clear night. There is a steady stream of oncoming traffic. The national speed limit applies. Which lights should you use?

Mark one answer

[a] Full beam headlights

[b] Sidelights

[c] Dipped headlights

[d] Fog lights

Question 11

You are following this lorry. You should keep well back from it to

Mark one answer

[a] give you a good view of the road ahead

[b] stop following traffic from rushing through the junction

[c] prevent traffic behind you from overtaking

[d] allow you to hurry through the traffic lights if they change

Question 12

You are driving behind a large goods vehicle. It signals left but steers to the right. You should

Mark one answer

ⓐ slow down and let the vehicle turn
ⓑ drive on, keeping to the left
ⓒ overtake on the right of it
ⓓ hold your speed and sound your horn

Question 13

You are following a vehicle on a wet road. You should leave a time gap of at least

Mark one answer

ⓐ one second
ⓑ two seconds
ⓒ three seconds
ⓓ four seconds

Question 14

You are driving along this road. The red van cuts in close in front of you. What should you do?

Mark one answer

ⓐ Accelerate to get closer to the red van
ⓑ Give a long blast on the horn
ⓒ Drop back to leave the correct separation distance
ⓓ Flash your headlights several times

Question 15

You are waiting in a traffic queue at night. To avoid dazzling following drivers you should

Mark one answer

ⓐ apply the handbrake only
ⓑ apply the footbrake only
ⓒ switch off your headlights
ⓓ use both the handbrake and footbrake

Question 16

You are driving in traffic at the speed limit for the road. The driver behind is trying to overtake. You should

Mark one answer

ⓐ move closer to the car ahead, so the driver behind has no room to overtake
ⓑ wave the driver behind to overtake when it is safe
ⓒ keep a steady course and allow the driver behind to overtake
ⓓ accelerate to get away from the driver behind

Question 17

You are driving at night on an unlit road following a slower-moving vehicle. You should

Mark one answer

ⓐ flash your headlights
ⓑ use dipped beam headlights
ⓒ switch off your headlights
ⓓ use full beam headlights

Question 18

A long, heavily-laden lorry is taking a long time to overtake you. What should you do?

Mark one answer

ⓐ Speed up
ⓑ Slow down
ⓒ Hold your speed
ⓓ Change direction

Question 19

You are using a slow-moving vehicle on a narrow winding road. You should

Mark one answer

ⓐ keep well out to stop vehicles overtaking dangerously
ⓑ wave following vehicles past you if you think they can overtake quickly
ⓒ pull in safely when you can, to let following vehicles overtake
ⓓ give a left signal when it is safe for vehicles to overtake you

Question 20

You are using a slow-moving vehicle on a narrow road. When traffic wishes to overtake you should

Mark one answer

ⓐ take no action
ⓑ put your hazard warning lights on
ⓒ stop immediately and wave it on
ⓓ pull in safely as soon as you can do so

Question 21

You are driving a slow-moving vehicle on a narrow winding road. In order to let other vehicles overtake you should

Mark one answer

ⓐ wave to them to pass
ⓑ pull in when you can
ⓒ show a left turn signal
ⓓ keep left and hold your speed

Question 22

You are riding a motorcycle and following a large vehicle at 40 mph. You should position yourself

Mark one answer

ⓐ close behind to make it easier to overtake the vehicle
ⓑ to the left of the road to make it easier to be seen
ⓒ close behind the vehicle to keep out of the wind
ⓓ well back so that you can see past the vehicle

Question 23

Which THREE of these emergency services might have blue flashing beacons?

Mark three answers

ⓐ Coastguard
ⓑ Bomb disposal
ⓒ Gritting lorries
ⓓ Animal ambulances
ⓔ Mountain rescue
ⓕ Doctors' cars

Question 24

A flashing green beacon on a vehicle means

Mark one answer

a) police on non-urgent duties

b) doctor on an emergency call

c) road safety patrol operating

d) gritting in progress

Question 25

Diamond-shaped signs give instructions to

Mark one answer

a) tram drivers

b) bus drivers

c) lorry drivers

d) taxi drivers

Question 26

Scooter riders should be especially careful when crossing tram lines because scooters have

Mark one answer

a) small engines

b) wide panniers

c) automatic gear boxes

d) narrow tyres

Question 27

On a road where trams operate, which of these vehicles will be most at risk from the tram rails?

Mark one answer

a) Cars

b) Cycles

c) Buses

d) Lorries

Question 28

A bus is stopped at a bus stop ahead of you. Its right-hand indicator is flashing. You should

Mark one answer

a) flash your headlights and slow down

b) slow down and give way if it is safe to do so

c) sound your horn and keep going

d) slow down and then sound your horn

Question 29

A bus lane on your left shows no times of operation. This means it is

Mark one answer

- a not in operation at all
- b only in operation at peak times
- c in operation 24 hours a day
- d only in operation in daylight hours

Question 30

You should ONLY flash your headlights to other road users

Mark one answer

- a to show that you are giving way
- b to show that you are about to reverse
- c to tell them that you have right of way
- d to let them know that you are there

Question 31

What should you use your horn for?

Mark one answer

- a To alert others to your presence
- b To allow you right of way
- c To greet other road users
- d To signal your annoyance

Question 32

A vehicle pulls out in front of you at a junction. What should you do?

Mark one answer

- a Swerve past it and sound your horn
- b Flash your headlights and drive up close behind
- c Slow down and be ready to stop
- d Accelerate past it immediately

Question 33

You are in a one-way street and want to turn right. You should position yourself

Mark one answer

- a in the right-hand lane
- b in the left-hand lane
- c in either lane, depending on the traffic
- d just left of the centre line

Question 34

You wish to turn right ahead. Why should you take up the correct position in good time?

Mark one answer

- a To allow other drivers to pull out in front of you
- b To give a better view into the road that you're joining
- c To help other road users know what you intend to do
- d To allow drivers to pass you on the right

Question 35

You are driving along a country road. A horse and rider are approaching. What should you do?

Mark two answers

ⓐ Increase your speed

ⓑ Sound your horn

ⓒ Flash your headlights

ⓓ Drive slowly past

ⓔ Give plenty of room

ⓕ Rev your engine

Question 36

A person herding sheep asks you to stop. You should

Mark one answer

ⓐ ignore them as they have no authority

ⓑ stop and switch off your engine

ⓒ continue on but drive slowly

ⓓ try and get past quickly

Question 37

When overtaking a horse and rider you should

Mark one answer

ⓐ sound your horn as a warning

ⓑ go past as quickly as possible

ⓒ flash your headlights as a warning

ⓓ go past slowly and carefully

Question 38

At a puffin crossing what colour follows the green signal?

Mark one answer

ⓐ Steady red

ⓑ Flashing amber

ⓒ Steady amber

ⓓ Flashing green

Question 39

You stop for pedestrians waiting to cross at a zebra crossing. They do not start to cross. What should you do?

Mark one answer

ⓐ Be patient and wait

ⓑ Sound your horn

ⓒ Carry on

ⓓ Wave them to cross

Question 40

You are riding on a country road. Two horses with riders are in the distance. You should

Mark one answer

ⓐ continue at your normal speed

ⓑ change down the gears quickly

ⓒ slow down and be ready to stop

ⓓ flash your headlight to warn them

Question 41

You should never wave people across at pedestrian crossings because

Mark one answer

ⓐ there may be another vehicle coming
ⓑ they may not be looking
ⓒ it is safer for you to carry on
ⓓ they may not be ready to cross

Question 42

At a pelican crossing the flashing amber light means you MUST

Mark one answer

ⓐ stop and wait for the green light
ⓑ stop and wait for the red light
ⓒ give way to pedestrians waiting to cross
ⓓ give way to pedestrians already on the crossing

Question 43

Following this vehicle too closely is unwise because

Mark one answer

ⓐ your brakes will overheat
ⓑ your view ahead is increased
ⓒ your engine will overheat
ⓓ your view ahead is reduced

Question 44

When riding a motorcycle your normal road position should allow

Mark two answers

ⓐ other vehicles to overtake on your left
ⓑ the driver ahead to see you in the mirrors
ⓒ you to prevent following vehicles from overtaking
ⓓ you to be seen by traffic that is emerging from junctions ahead
ⓔ you to ride within half a metre (1 foot 8ins) of the kerb

Question 45

You are in a line of traffic. The driver behind you is following very closely. What action should you take?

Mark one answer

ⓐ Ignore the following driver and continue to drive within the speed limit
ⓑ Slow down, gradually increasing the gap between you and the vehicle in front
ⓒ Signal left and wave the following driver past
ⓓ Move over to a position just left of the centre line of the road

Question 46

You are travelling at the legal speed limit. A vehicle comes up quickly behind, flashing its headlights. You should

Mark one answer

- ⓐ accelerate to make a gap behind you
- ⓑ touch the brakes sharply to show your brake lights
- ⓒ maintain your speed to prevent the vehicle from overtaking
- ⓓ allow the vehicle to overtake

Question 47

Which of the following vehicles will use blue flashing beacons?

Mark three answers

- ⓐ Motorway maintenance
- ⓑ Bomb disposal
- ⓒ Blood transfusion
- ⓓ Police patrol
- ⓔ Breakdown recovery

Question 48

When being followed by an ambulance showing a flashing blue beacon you should

Mark one answer

- ⓐ pull over as soon as safely possible to let it pass
- ⓑ accelerate hard to get away from it
- ⓒ maintain your speed and course
- ⓓ brake harshly and immediately stop in the road

Question 49

What type of emergency vehicle is fitted with a green flashing beacon?

Mark one answer

- ⓐ Fire engine
- ⓑ Road gritter
- ⓒ Ambulance
- ⓓ Doctor's car

Question 50

A vehicle has a flashing green beacon. What does this mean?

Mark one answer

- ⓐ A doctor is answering an emergency call
- ⓑ The vehicle is slow-moving
- ⓒ It is a motorway police patrol vehicle
- ⓓ A vehicle is carrying hazardous chemicals

Question 51

At which type of crossing are cyclists allowed to ride across with pedestrians?

Mark one answer

- ⓐ Toucan
- ⓑ Puffin
- ⓒ Pelican
- ⓓ Zebra

Answers and explanations

Q001 b

Q002 a You must give way to pedestrians already on the crossing but may drive on if the crossing is clear.

Q003 b

Q004 b

Q005 a

Q006 b

Q007 b A two-second time gap from the vehicle in front provides a safe gap in good conditions.

Q008 b

Q009 c

Q010 c

Q011 a The nearer you are to a lorry, the less you can see ahead.

Q012 a

Q013 d In good conditions you should allow two seconds but on a wet road you double this to four.

Q014 c

Q015 a Using the footbrake would activate your brake lights and might dazzle following drivers.

Q016 c

Q017 b

Q018 b By slowing down, you allow the lorry to get past, which is the only safe option.

Q019 c 'a' and 'b' are dangerous and 'd' is confusing. Other drivers might think you are stopping or turning left.

Q020 d

Q021 b

Q022 d If you can see past the vehicle you can decide whether it is safe to overtake.

Q023 a,b,e

Q024 b

Q025 a

Q026 d

Q027 b

Q028 b

Q029 c

Q030 d You should only flash your headlights to warn other road users that you are there.

Q031 a

Q032 c This is the only safe thing to do. The other answers are the actions of an aggressive driver.

Q033 a To turn right from a one-way street you normally position yourself in the right-hand lane.

Q034 c The position of your car helps signal your intentions to other drivers.

Q035 d,e

Q036 b

Answers and explanations

Q037 d

Q038 c

Q039 a Pedestrians are naturally nervous and cautious at crossings, so allow them time. Only drive on if you are certain they do not intend to cross.

Q040 c Take extra care where there are horses around as they can easily be alarmed.

Q041 a

Q042 d

Q043 d If you hang back you will have a much better view of the road ahead.

Q044 b,d
Motorcycles are easily missed by other road users. It is important that you make sure other drivers can see you.

Q045 b By increasing the gap between you and the vehicle in front, you give yourself and the driver behind more room to stop should you need it.

Q046 d This is your only safe option.

Q047 b,c,d

Q048 a

Q049 d Doctors on emergency call may display a flashing green beacon. Slow-moving vehicles have amber flashing beacons. Police, fire and ambulance service vehicles have blue flashing beacons.

Q050 a

Q051 a

Driving Theory
Test
Questions
2000/2001

Safety & Your Vehicle

BSM
We won't fail you

Question 1

When riding a different motorcycle you should

Mark one answer

ⓐ ask someone to ride with you for the first time

ⓑ ride as soon as possible as all controls and switches are the same

ⓒ leave your gloves behind so switches can be operated easier at first

ⓓ be sure you know where all controls and switches are

Question 2

When should you especially check the engine oil level?

Mark one answer

ⓐ Before a long journey

ⓑ When the engine is hot

ⓒ Early in the morning

ⓓ Every 6000 miles

Question 3

Which of these, if allowed to get low, could cause an accident?

Mark one answer

ⓐ Antifreeze level

ⓑ Brake fluid level

ⓒ Battery water level

ⓓ Radiator coolant level

Question 4

Which FOUR of these MUST be in good working order for your car to be roadworthy?

Mark four answers

ⓐ Temperature gauge

ⓑ Speedometer

ⓒ Windscreen washers

ⓓ Windscreen wiper

ⓔ Oil warning light

ⓕ Horn

Question 5

A loose drive chain on a motorcycle could cause

Mark one answer

ⓐ the front wheel to wobble

ⓑ the ignition to cut out

ⓒ the brakes to fail

ⓓ the rear wheel to lock

Question 6

A wrongly adjusted drive chain can

Mark three answers

ⓐ cause an accident

ⓑ make wheels wobble

ⓒ create a noisy rattle

ⓓ affect gear changing

ⓔ cause a suspension fault

Question 7

Which THREE does the law require you to keep in good condition?

Mark three answers

- a Gears
- b Transmission
- c Headlights
- d Windscreen
- e Seat belts

Question 8

New petrol-engined cars must be fitted with catalytic converters. The reason for this is to

Mark one answer

- a control exhaust noise levels
- b prolong the life of the exhaust system
- c allow the exhaust system to be recycled
- d reduce harmful exhaust emissions

Question 9

Which TWO are badly affected if the tyres are under-inflated?

Mark two answers

- a Braking
- b Steering
- c Changing gear
- d Parking

Question 10

What can cause heavy steering?

Mark one answer

- a Driving on ice
- b Badly worn brakes
- c Over-inflated tyres
- d Under-inflated tyres

Question 11

What is the most important reason why you should keep your motorcycle regularly maintained?

Mark one answer

- a To accelerate faster than other traffic
- b So the motorcycle can carry panniers
- c To keep the machine roadworthy
- d So the motorcycle can carry a passenger

Question 12

It is essential that tyre pressures are checked regularly. When should this be done?

Mark one answer

- a After any lengthy journey
- b After travelling at high speed
- c When tyres are hot
- d When tyres are cold

Question 13

How often should motorcycle tyre pressures be checked?

Mark one answer

a Only during each regular service
b After each long journey
c At least monthly
d At least weekly

Question 14

Driving with under-inflated tyres can affect

Mark two answers

a engine temperature
b fuel consumption
c braking
d oil pressure

Question 15

The legal minimum depth of tread for motorcycle tyres is

Mark one answer

a 1 mm
b 1.6 mm
c 2.5 mm
d 4 mm

Question 16

Your motorcycle has tubed tyres fitted as standard. When replacing a tyre you should

Mark one answer

a replace the tube if it is 6 months old
b replace the tube if it has covered 6,000 miles
c replace the tube only if replacing the rear tyre
d replace the tube with each change of tyre

Question 17

You are riding a machine of more than 50cc. Which FOUR would make a tyre illegal?

Mark four answers

a Tread less than 1.6 mm deep
b Tread less than 1 mm deep
c A large bulge in the wall
d A recut tread
e Exposed ply or cord
f A stone wedged in the tread

Question 18

It is illegal to drive with tyres that

Mark one answer

a have been bought second-hand
b have a large deep cut in the side wall
c are of different makes
d are of different tread patterns

Question 19

The legal minimum depth of tread for car tyres over three quarters of the breadth is

Mark one answer

ⓐ 1 mm

ⓑ 1.6 mm

ⓒ 2.5 mm

ⓓ 4 mm

Question 20

How should you ride a motorcycle when NEW tyres have just been fitted?

Mark one answer

ⓐ Carefully, until the shiny surface is worn off

ⓑ By braking hard especially into bends

ⓒ Through normal riding with higher air pressures

ⓓ By riding at faster than normal speeds

Question 21

Excessive or uneven tyre wear can be caused by faults in the

Mark two answers

ⓐ gearbox

ⓑ braking system

ⓒ suspension

ⓓ exhaust system

Question 22

Your vehicle pulls to one side when braking. You should

Mark one answer

ⓐ change the tyres around

ⓑ consult your garage as soon as possible

ⓒ pump the pedal when braking

ⓓ use your handbrake at the same time

Question 23

The main cause of brake fade is

Mark one answer

ⓐ the brakes overheating

ⓑ air in the brake fluid

ⓒ oil on the brakes

ⓓ the brakes out of adjustment

Question 24

Your anti-lock brakes warning light stays on. You should

Mark one answer

ⓐ check the brake fluid level

ⓑ check the footbrake free play

ⓒ check that the handbrake is released

ⓓ have the brakes checked immediately

Question 25

You should maintain cable operated brakes

Mark two answers

a) by regular adjustment when necessary
b) at normal service times only
c) yearly, before taking the machine for its MOT
d) by oiling cables and pivots regularly

Question 26

What does this instrument panel light mean when lit?

Mark one answer

a) Gear lever in park
b) Gear lever in neutral
c) Handbrake on
d) Handbrake off

Question 27

When MUST you use dipped headlights during the day?

Mark one answer

a) All the time
b) Along narrow streets
c) In poor visibility
d) When parking

Question 28

Which instrument panel warning light would show that headlights are on full beam?

Mark one answer

a)   b)

c)   d)

Question 29

While driving, this warning light on your dashboard comes on. It means

Mark one answer

a) a fault in the braking system
b) the engine oil is low
c) a rear light has failed
d) your seat belt is not fastened

Question 30

You are driving on a motorway. The traffic ahead is braking sharply because of an accident. How could you warn following traffic?

Mark one answer

- a Briefly use the hazard warning lights
- b Switch on the hazard warning lights continuously
- c Briefly use the rear fog lights
- d Switch on the headlights continuously

Question 31

When may you use hazard warning lights?

Mark one answer

- a To park alongside another car
- b To park on double yellow lines
- c When you are being towed
- d When you have broken down

Question 32

Hazard warning lights should be used when vehicles are

Mark one answer

- a broken down and causing an obstruction
- b faulty and moving slowly
- c being towed along a road
- d reversing into a side road

Question 33

It is important to wear suitable shoes when you are driving. Why is this?

Mark one answer

- a To prevent wear on the pedals
- b To maintain control of the pedals
- c To enable you to adjust your seat
- d To enable you to walk for assistance if you break down

Question 34

A properly adjusted head restraint will

Mark one answer

- a make you more comfortable
- b help you to avoid neck injury
- c help you to relax
- d help you to maintain your driving position

Question 35

What will reduce the risk of neck injury resulting from a collision?

Mark one answer

- a An air-sprung seat
- b Anti-lock brakes
- c A collapsible steering wheel
- d A properly adjusted head restraint

Question 36

How can you, as a driver, help the environment?

Mark three answers

(a) By reducing your speed
(b) By gentle acceleration
(c) By using leaded fuel
(d) By driving faster
(e) By harsh acceleration
(f) By servicing your vehicle properly

Question 37

To help the environment, you can avoid wasting fuel by

Mark three answers

(a) having your vehicle properly serviced
(b) making sure your tyres are correctly inflated
(c) not over-revving in the lower gears
(d) driving at higher speeds where possible
(e) keeping an empty roof rack properly fitted
(f) servicing your vehicle less regularly

Question 38

Why do MOT tests include a strict exhaust emission test?

Mark one answer

(a) To recover the cost of expensive garage equipment
(b) To help protect the environment against pollution
(c) To discover which fuel supplier is used the most
(d) To make sure diesel and petrol engines emit the same fumes

Question 39

Which THREE things can you, as a road user, do to help the environment?

Mark three answers

(a) Cycle when possible
(b) Drive on under-inflated tyres
(c) Use the choke for as long as possible on a cold engine
(d) Have your vehicle properly tuned and serviced
(e) Watch the traffic and plan ahead
(f) Brake as late as possible without skidding

Question 40

As a driver you can cause MORE damage to the environment by

Mark three answers

- a. choosing a fuel efficient vehicle
- b. making a lot of short journeys
- c. driving in as high a gear as possible
- d. accelerating as quickly as possible
- e. having your vehicle regularly serviced
- f. using leaded fuel

Question 41

Motor vehicles can harm the environment. This has resulted in

Mark three answers

- a. air pollution
- b. damage to buildings
- c. reduced health risks
- d. improved public transport
- e. less use of electrical vehicles
- f. using up natural resources

Question 42

To reduce the damage your vehicle causes to the environment you should

Mark three answers

- a. use narrow side streets
- b. avoid harsh acceleration
- c. brake in good time
- d. anticipate well ahead
- e. use busy routes

Question 43

To help protect the environment you should NOT

Mark one answer

- a. remove your roof rack when unloaded
- b. use your car for very short journeys
- c. walk, cycle, or use public transport
- d. empty the boot of unnecessary weight

Question 44

You service your own vehicle. How should you get rid of the old engine oil?

Mark one answer

- a. Take it to a local authority site
- b. Pour it down a drain
- c. Tip it into a hole in the ground
- d. Put it into your dustbin

Question 45

Which of the following would NOT make you more visible in daylight?

Mark one answer

- a. A black helmet
- b. A white helmet
- c. Switching on your dipped headlamp
- d. Wearing a fluorescent jacket

Question 46

When riding and wearing brightly coloured clothing you will

Mark one answer

ⓐ dazzle other motorists on the road

ⓑ be seen more easily by other motorists

ⓒ create a hazard by distracting other drivers

ⓓ be able to ride on unlit roads at night with sidelights

Question 47

You are riding a motorcycle in very hot weather. You should

Mark one answer

ⓐ ride with your visor fully open

ⓑ continue to wear protective clothing

ⓒ wear trainers instead of boots

ⓓ slacken your helmet strap

Question 48

Why should you wear fluorescent clothing when riding in daylight?

Mark one answer

ⓐ It reduces wind resistance

ⓑ It prevents injury if you come off the machine

ⓒ It helps other road users to see you

ⓓ It keeps you cool in hot weather

Question 49

Why should riders wear reflective clothing?

Mark one answer

ⓐ To protect them from the cold

ⓑ To protect them from direct sunlight

ⓒ To be seen better in daylight

ⓓ To be seen better at night

Question 50

Which of the following make it easier for motorcyclists to be seen?

Mark three answers

ⓐ Using a dipped headlight

ⓑ Wearing a fluorescent jacket

ⓒ Wearing a white helmet

ⓓ Wearing a grey helmet

ⓔ Wearing black leathers

ⓕ Using a tinted visor

Question 51

You are carrying two 13-year-old children and their parents in your car. Who is responsible for seeing that the children wear seat belts?

Mark one answer

ⓐ The children's parents

ⓑ You, the driver

ⓒ The front-seat passenger

ⓓ The children

Question 52

You are driving a friend's children home from school. They are both under 14 years old. Who is responsible for making sure they wear a seat belt?

Mark one answer

ⓐ An adult passenger

ⓑ The children

ⓒ You, the driver

ⓓ Your friend

Question 53

Car passengers MUST wear a seat belt if one is available, unless they are

Mark one answer

ⓐ under 14 years old

ⓑ under 1.5 metres (5 feet) in height

ⓒ sitting in the rear seat

ⓓ exempt for medical reasons

Question 54

Excessive or uneven tyre wear can be caused by faults in which THREE?

Mark three answers

ⓐ The gearbox

ⓑ The braking system

ⓒ The accelerator

ⓓ The exhaust system

ⓔ Wheel alignment

ⓕ The suspension

Question 55

Which of the following fairings would give you the best weather protection?

Mark one answer

ⓐ Handlebar

ⓑ Sports

ⓒ Touring

ⓓ Windscreen

Question 56

It would be illegal to ride WITH a helmet on when

Mark one answer

ⓐ the helmet is not fastened correctly

ⓑ the helmet is more than four years old

ⓒ you have borrowed someone else's helmet

ⓓ the helmet does not have chin protection

Question 57

Your safety helmet has a small crack. You should

Mark one answer

ⓐ get a new one before riding

ⓑ ride at low speeds only

ⓒ ask the police to inspect it

ⓓ have it repaired by an expert

Question 58

Your visor becomes badly scratched. You should

Mark one answer

ⓐ polish it with a fine abrasive
ⓑ replace it
ⓒ wash it in soapy water
ⓓ clean it with petrol

Question 59

You want to ride your motorcycle in the dark. What could you wear to be seen more easily?

Mark two answers

ⓐ A black leather jacket
ⓑ Reflective clothing
ⓒ A white helmet
ⓓ A red helmet

Question 60

You are testing your suspension. You notice that your vehicle keeps bouncing when you press down on the front wing. What does this mean?

Mark one answer

ⓐ Worn tyres
ⓑ Tyres under-inflated
ⓒ Steering wheel not located centrally
ⓓ Worn shock absorbers

Question 61

Which TWO of the following will improve fuel consumption?

Mark two answers

ⓐ Reducing your road speed
ⓑ Planning well ahead
ⓒ Late and harsh braking
ⓓ Driving in lower gears
ⓔ Short journeys with a cold engine
ⓕ Rapid acceleration

Question 62

Which THREE of the following are most likely to waste fuel?

Mark three answers

ⓐ Reducing your speed
ⓑ Carrying unnecessary weight
ⓒ Using the wrong grade of fuel
ⓓ Under-inflated tyres
ⓔ Using different brands of fuel
ⓕ A fitted, empty roof rack

Question 63

You have a loose filler cap on your diesel fuel tank. This will

Mark two answers

ⓐ waste fuel and money
ⓑ make roads slippery for other road users
ⓒ improve your vehicle's fuel consumption
ⓓ increase the level of exhaust emissions

Question 64

To avoid spillage after refuelling, you should make sure that

Mark one answer

ⓐ your tank is only 3/4 full
ⓑ you have used a locking filler cap
ⓒ you check your fuel gauge is working
ⓓ your filler cap is securely fastened

Question 65

Extra care should be taken when refuelling, because diesel fuel when spilt is

Mark one answer

ⓐ sticky
ⓑ odourless
ⓒ clear
ⓓ slippery

Question 66

You must NOT sound your horn

Mark one answer

ⓐ between 10 pm and 6 am in a built-up area
ⓑ at any time in a built-up area
ⓒ between 11.30 pm and 7 am in a built-up area
ⓓ between 11.30 pm and 6 am on any road

Question 67

When should you NOT use your horn in a built-up area?

Mark one answer

ⓐ Between 8 pm and 8 am
ⓑ Between 9 pm and dawn
ⓒ Between dusk and 8 am
ⓓ Between 11.30 pm and 7 am

Question 68

Why are mirrors often slightly curved (convex)?

Mark one answer

ⓐ They give a wider field of vision
ⓑ They totally cover blind spots
ⓒ They make it easier to judge the speed of following traffic
ⓓ They make following traffic look bigger

Question 69

You cannot see clearly behind when reversing. What should you do?

Mark one answer

ⓐ Open your window to look behind
ⓑ Open the door and look behind
ⓒ Look in the nearside mirror
ⓓ Ask someone to guide you

Question 70

Why can it be helpful to have mirrors fitted on each side of your motorcycle?

Mark one answer

- ⓐ To judge the gap when filtering in traffic
- ⓑ To give protection when riding in poor weather
- ⓒ To make your machine appear larger to other drivers
- ⓓ To give you the best view of the road behind

Question 71

When MUST you use a dipped headlight during the day?

Mark one answer

- ⓐ On country roads
- ⓑ In poor visibility
- ⓒ Along narrow streets
- ⓓ When parking

Question 72

Your side stand is not raised fully when you start to ride. What could this do?

Mark one answer

- ⓐ Alter the machine's centre of gravity
- ⓑ Catch on your feet
- ⓒ Dig into the ground when you are cornering
- ⓓ Cause the machine to steer badly

Question 73

What is most likely to cause high fuel consumption?

Mark one answer

- ⓐ Poor steering control
- ⓑ Accelerating around bends
- ⓒ Staying in high gears
- ⓓ Harsh braking and accelerating

Question 74

A properly serviced vehicle will give

Mark two answers

- ⓐ lower insurance premiums
- ⓑ you a refund on your road tax
- ⓒ better fuel economy
- ⓓ cleaner exhaust emissions

Question 75

Driving at 70 mph uses more fuel than driving at 50 mph by up to

Mark one answer

- ⓐ 10%
- ⓑ 30%
- ⓒ 75%
- ⓓ 100%

Question 76

When driving a car fitted with automatic transmission what would you use 'kick down' for?

Mark one answer

- ⓐ Cruise control
- ⓑ Quick acceleration
- ⓒ Slow braking
- ⓓ Fuel economy

Question 77

When a roof rack is not in use it should be removed. Why is this?

Mark one answer

- ⓐ It will affect the suspension
- ⓑ It is illegal
- ⓒ It will affect your braking
- ⓓ It will waste fuel

Question 78

A roof rack fitted to your car will

Mark one answer

- ⓐ reduce fuel consumption
- ⓑ improve the road handling
- ⓒ make your car go faster
- ⓓ increase fuel consumption

Question 79

The pictured vehicle is 'environmentally friendly' because it

Mark three answers

- ⓐ reduces noise pollution
- ⓑ uses diesel fuel
- ⓒ uses electricity
- ⓓ uses unleaded fuel
- ⓔ reduces parking spaces
- ⓕ reduces town traffic

Question 80

Supertrams or Light Rapid Transit (LRT) systems are environmentally friendly because

Mark one answer

- ⓐ they use diesel power
- ⓑ they use quieter roads
- ⓒ they use electric power
- ⓓ they do not operate during rush hour

Question 81

'Red routes' in major cities have been introduced to

Mark one answer

a) raise the speed limits

b) help the traffic flow

c) provide better parking

d) allow lorries to load more freely

Question 82

To reduce the volume of traffic on the roads you could

Mark three answers

a) use public transport more often

b) share a car when possible

c) walk or cycle on short journeys

d) travel by car at all times

e) use a car with a smaller engine

f) drive in a bus lane

Question 83

In some narrow residential streets you will find a speed limit of

Mark one answer

a) 20 mph

b) 25 mph

c) 35 mph

d) 40 mph

Question 84

Road humps, chicanes, and narrowings are

Mark one answer

a) always at major road works

b) used to increase traffic speed

c) at toll-bridge approaches only

d) traffic calming measures

Question 85

You enter a road where there are road humps. What should you do?

Mark one answer

a) Maintain a reduced speed throughout

b) Accelerate quickly between each one

c) Always keep to the maximum legal speed

d) Drive slowly at school times only

Question 86

A motorcyclist may only carry a pillion passenger when

Mark three answers

- ⓐ the rider has successfully completed CBT (Compulsory Basic Training)
- ⓑ the rider holds a full licence for the category of machine
- ⓒ the motorcycle is fitted with rear foot pegs
- ⓓ the rider has a full car licence and is over 21
- ⓔ there is a proper passenger seat fitted
- ⓕ there is no sidecar fitted to the machine

Question 87

On your vehicle, where would you find a catalytic converter?

Mark one answer

- ⓐ In the fuel tank
- ⓑ In the air filter
- ⓒ On the cooling system
- ⓓ On the exhaust system

Question 88

For which TWO of these may you use hazard warning lights?

Mark two answers

- ⓐ When travelling on a motorway, to warn drivers behind of a hazard ahead
- ⓑ When you are double parked on a two-way road
- ⓒ When your direction indicators are not working
- ⓓ When warning oncoming traffic that you intend to stop
- ⓔ When your vehicle has broken down and is causing an obstruction

Question 89

Daytime visibility is poor but not seriously reduced. You should switch on

Mark one answer

- ⓐ headlights and fog lights
- ⓑ front fog lights
- ⓒ dipped headlights
- ⓓ rear fog lights

Question 90

Why are vehicles fitted with rear fog lights?

Mark one answer

ⓐ To be seen when driving at high speed

ⓑ To use if broken down in a dangerous position

ⓒ To make them more visible in thick fog

ⓓ To warn drivers following closely to drop back

Question 91

Tyre pressures should be increased on your motorcycle when

Mark one answer

ⓐ riding on a wet road

ⓑ carrying a pillion passenger

ⓒ travelling on an uneven surface

ⓓ riding on twisty roads

Question 92

Your oil light comes on as you are riding. You should

Mark one answer

ⓐ go to a dealer for an oil change

ⓑ go to the nearest garage for their advice

ⓒ ride slowly for a few miles to see if the light goes out

ⓓ stop as quickly as possible and try to find the cause

Question 93

When may you have to increase the tyre pressures on your motorcycle?

Mark three answers

ⓐ When carrying a pillion passenger

ⓑ After a long journey

ⓒ When carrying a heavy load

ⓓ When riding at high speeds

ⓔ When riding in hot weather

Question 94

Which TWO of these items on a motorcycle MUST be kept clean?

Mark two answers

ⓐ Number plate

ⓑ Wheels

ⓒ Engine

ⓓ Fairing

ⓔ Headlights

Question 95

Motorcycle tyres MUST

Mark two answers

ⓐ have the same tread pattern

ⓑ be correctly inflated

ⓒ be the same size, front and rear

ⓓ both be the same make

ⓔ have sufficient tread depth

Question 96

You are riding on a wet road. When braking you should

Mark one answer

a) apply the rear brake well before the front

b) apply the front brake just before the rear

c) avoid using the front brake at all

d) avoid using the rear brake at all

Question 97

You should use the engine cut-out switch on your motorcycle to

Mark one answer

a) save wear and tear on the battery

b) stop the engine on short stops

c) stop the engine in an emergency

d) save wear and tear on the ignition

Question 98

Riding your motorcycle with a slack or worn drive chain may cause

Mark one answer

a) an engine misfire

b) early tyre wear

c) increased emissions

d) a locked wheel

Question 99

You have adjusted the drive chain tension. You should check the

Mark one answer

a) rear wheel alignment

b) tyre pressures

c) valve clearances

d) sidelights

Question 100

As a driver you can help reduce pollution levels in town centres by

Mark one answer

a) driving more quickly

b) using leaded fuel

c) walking or cycling

d) driving short journeys

Question 101

You will use more fuel if you drive your vehicle with tyres that are

Mark one answer

a) under-inflated

b) of different makes

c) over-inflated

d) new and hardly used

Question 102

How should you dispose of a used vehicle battery?

Mark two answers

ⓐ Take it to a local authority site
ⓑ Put it in the dustbin
ⓒ Break it up into pieces
ⓓ Leave it on waste land
ⓔ Take it to a garage
ⓕ Burn it on a fire

Question 103

The purpose of a catalytic converter is to reduce

Mark one answer

ⓐ fuel consumption
ⓑ the risk of fire
ⓒ toxic exhaust gases
ⓓ engine wear

Question 104

Which of these fuels should be used in a vehicle fitted with a catalytic converter?

Mark one answer

ⓐ Leaded petrol
ⓑ Propane gas
ⓒ Butane gas
ⓓ Unleaded petrol

Question 105

Unbalanced wheels on a car may cause

Mark one answer

ⓐ the steering to pull to one side
ⓑ the steering to vibrate
ⓒ the brakes to fail
ⓓ the tyres to deflate

Question 106

Turning the steering wheel while your car is stationary can cause damage to the

Mark two answers

ⓐ gearbox
ⓑ engine
ⓒ brakes
ⓓ steering
ⓔ tyres

Question 107

Your vehicle has a catalytic converter. Its purpose is to reduce

Mark one answer

ⓐ exhaust noise
ⓑ fuel consumption
ⓒ exhaust emissions
ⓓ engine noise

Question 108

Catalytic converters are fitted to make the

Mark one answer

ⓐ engine produce more power
ⓑ exhaust system easier to replace
ⓒ engine run quietly
ⓓ exhaust fumes cleaner

Answers and explanations

Q001 d
Q002 a
Q003 b A low level of brake fluid may cause your brakes to fail.
Q004 b,c,d,f These must, by law, be in good working order.
Q005 d Drive chains require frequent adjustment and lubrication. If the chain is loose it can jump off the sprocket and lock the rear wheel.
Q006 a,c,d
Q007 c,d,e
Q008 d This helps the car operate more efficiently and cause less air pollution. Only unleaded fuel may be used.
Q009 a,b
Q010 d
Q011 c
Q012 d
Q013 d
Q014 b,c
Q015 a
Q016 d A punctured tyre should be properly repaired or replaced and if you have tubed tyres this means replacing the inner tyre as well.

Q017 b,c,d,e
Q018 b
Q019 b
Q020 a New tyres have a shiny surface which can reduce the grip. You need to ride carefully until the shiny surface is worn off. This could take up to 100 miles.
Q021 b,c
Q022 b
Q023 a
Q024 d
Q025 a,d
Q026 c
Q027 c
Q028 a
Q029 a
Q030 a
Q031 d You should not use hazard warning lights when being towed so 'c' is wrong.
Q032 a
Q033 b
Q034 b
Q035 d If you are involved in an accident, the head restraint helps protect your neck from whiplash.
Q036 a,b,f

Answers and explanations

Q037　a,b,c

Q038　b

Q039　a,d,e

Q040　b,d,f
A lot of short journeys use up a lot of petrol and pollute the atmosphere with the exhaust fumes.

Q041　a,b,f

Q042　b,c,d
Doing these make for smoother driving which uses less fuel and so cuts down on pollution.

Q043　b

Q044　a

Q045　a

Q046　b

Q047　b Protective clothing offers you protection from some kinds of injury.

Q048　c

Q049　d

Q050　a,b,c

Q051　b

Q052　c

Q053　d All passengers, front and rear, must wear seat belts, if fitted, unless exempt for medical reasons.

Q054　b,e,f

Q055　c

Q056　a

Q057　a

Q058　b A badly scratched visor can distort your vision, causing dazzle from oncoming headlights at night and glare from a low winter sun.

Q059　b,c

Q060　d

Q061　a,b

Q062　b,d,f

Q063　a,b

Q064　d

Q065　d

Q066　c The regulation only applies in a built up area.

Q067　d

Q068　a Convex mirrors give a wider field of vision but also make traffic look further away than it really is, so you need to use them with care.

Q069　d If you cannot see properly you need to get someone to help.

Q070　d

Q071　b

Q072　c This could cause an accident.

Answers and explanations

Q073 d Harsh braking is one of
         the major causes of high
         fuel consumption.

Q074 c,d

Q075 b

Q076 b A short, firm pressure
         right down on the gas pedal
         causes a quick change down
         to the next lower gear –
         useful, for example, when
         you need to overtake.

Q077 d

Q078 d

Q079 a,c,f

Q080 c

Q081 b

Q082 a,b,c

Q083 a This is a traffic calming
         measure.

Q084 d

Q085 a Road humps are there to slow
         the traffic in residential areas.

Q086 b,c,e

Q087 d

Q088 a,e

Q089 c

Q090 c If visibility drops below
         about 100 metres (328 feet)
         use fog lights.

Q091 b Inflate the tyres according to
         the maker's instruction.

Q092 d

Q093 a,c,d

Q094 a,e

Q095 b,e

Q096 b You need to apply a more
         equal pressure to the front
         and rear brakes than you
         would in good road and
         weather conditions.

Q097 c

Q098 d

Q099 a

Q100 c

Q101 a

Q102 a,e

Q103 c

Q104 d

Q105 b

Q106 d,e

Q107 c

Q108 d

Driving Theory
Test
Questions

2000/2001

Safety Margins

We won't fail you

Question 1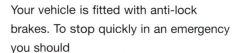

Your vehicle is fitted with anti-lock brakes. To stop quickly in an emergency you should

Mark one answer

- ⓐ brake firmly and pump the brake pedal on and off
- ⓑ brake rapidly and firmly without releasing the brake pedal
- ⓒ brake gently and pump the brake pedal on and off
- ⓓ brake rapidly once, and immediately release the brake pedal

Question 2

Your car is fitted with anti-lock brakes. You need to stop in an emergency. You should

Mark one answer

- ⓐ brake normally and avoid turning the steering wheel
- ⓑ press the brake pedal rapidly and firmly until you have stopped
- ⓒ keep pushing and releasing the foot brake quickly to prevent skidding
- ⓓ apply the handbrake to reduce the stopping distance

Question 3

You are driving a vehicle fitted with anti-lock brakes. You need to stop in an emergency. You should apply the footbrake

Mark one answer

- ⓐ slowly and gently
- ⓑ slowly but firmly
- ⓒ rapidly and gently
- ⓓ rapidly and firmly

Question 4

Anti-lock brakes reduce the chances of a skid occurring particularly when

Mark one answer

- ⓐ driving down steep hills
- ⓑ braking during normal driving
- ⓒ braking in an emergency
- ⓓ driving on good road surfaces

Question 5

Your vehicle has anti-lock brakes, but they may not always prevent skidding. This is most likely to happen when driving

Mark two answers

- ⓐ in foggy conditions
- ⓑ on surface water
- ⓒ on loose road surfaces
- ⓓ on dry tarmac
- ⓔ at night on unlit roads

Question 6

Anti-lock brakes prevent wheels from locking. This means the tyres are less likely to

Mark one answer

ⓐ aquaplane

ⓑ skid

ⓒ puncture

ⓓ wear

Question 7

Anti-lock brakes are most effective when you

Mark one answer

ⓐ keep pumping the foot brake to prevent skidding

ⓑ brake normally, but grip the steering wheel tightly

ⓒ brake rapidly and firmly until you have slowed down

ⓓ apply the handbrake to reduce the stopping distance

Question 8

Vehicles fitted with anti-lock brakes

Mark one answer

ⓐ are impossible to skid

ⓑ can be steered while you are braking

ⓒ accelerate much faster

ⓓ are not fitted with a handbrake

Question 9

Anti-lock brakes may not work as effectively if the road surface is

Mark two answers

ⓐ dry

ⓑ loose

ⓒ wet

ⓓ good

ⓔ firm

Question 10

Anti-lock brakes are of most use when you are

Mark one answer

ⓐ braking gently

ⓑ driving on worn tyres

ⓒ braking excessively

ⓓ driving normally

Question 11

Driving a vehicle fitted with anti-lock brakes allows you to

Mark one answer

ⓐ brake harder because it is impossible to skid

ⓑ drive at higher speeds

ⓒ steer and brake at the same time

ⓓ pay less attention to the road ahead

Question 12

When would an anti-lock braking system start to work?

Mark one answer

- ⓐ After the parking brake has been applied
- ⓑ Whenever pressure on the brake pedal is applied
- ⓒ Just as the wheels are about to lock
- ⓓ When the normal braking system fails to operate

Question 13

Anti-lock brakes will take effect when

Mark one answer

- ⓐ you do not brake quickly enough
- ⓑ excessive brake pressure has been applied
- ⓒ you have not seen a hazard ahead
- ⓓ speeding on slippery road surfaces

Question 14

Anti-lock brakes can greatly assist with

Mark one answer

- ⓐ a higher cruising speed
- ⓑ steering control when braking
- ⓒ control when accelerating
- ⓓ motorway driving

Question 15

You are on a good, dry road surface and your vehicle has good brakes and tyres. What is the overall stopping distance at 40 mph?

Mark one answer

- ⓐ 23 metres (75 feet)
- ⓑ 36 metres (118 feet)
- ⓒ 53 metres (175 feet)
- ⓓ 96 metres (315 feet)

Question 16

You are on a good, dry road surface. Your vehicle has good brakes and tyres. What is the braking distance at 50 mph?

Mark one answer

- ⓐ 38 metres (125 feet)
- ⓑ 14 metres (46 feet)
- ⓒ 24 metres (79 feet)
- ⓓ 55 metres (180 feet)

Question 17

Your overall stopping distance will be longer when riding

Mark one answer

- ⓐ at night
- ⓑ in the fog
- ⓒ with a passenger
- ⓓ up a hill

Question 18

You are riding a motorcycle in good road conditions. The most effective way to use the brakes is to

Mark one answer

[a] apply both brakes with greater pressure on the rear

[b] apply both brakes with equal pressure

[c] apply the rear brake first and the front just before you stop

[d] apply both brakes with greater pressure on the front

Question 19

What is the shortest stopping distance at 70 mph?

Mark one answer

[a] 53 metres (175 feet)

[b] 60 metres (197 feet)

[c] 73 metres (240 feet)

[d] 96 metres (315 feet)

Question 20

You are travelling at 50 mph on a good, dry road. What is your shortest overall stopping distance?

Mark one answer

[a] 36 metres (120 feet)

[b] 53 metres (175 feet)

[c] 75 metres (245 feet)

[d] 96 metres (315 feet)

Question 21

What is the shortest overall stopping distance on a dry road from 60 mph?

Mark one answer

[a] 53 metres (175 feet)

[b] 58 metres (190 feet)

[c] 73 metres (240 feet)

[d] 96 metres (315 feet)

Question 22

When driving in fog, which of the following are correct?

Mark three answers

[a] Use dipped headlights

[b] Use headlights on full beam

[c] Allow more time for your journey

[d] Keep close to the car in front

[e] Slow down

[f] Use side lights only

Question 23

"Only a fool breaks the Two-Second Rule" refers to

Mark one answer

[a] the time recommended when using the choke

[b] the separation distance when riding in good conditions

[c] restarting a stalled engine in busy traffic

[d] the time you should keep your foot down at a junction

Question 24

You are on a fast, open road in good conditions. For safety, the distance between you and the vehicle in front should be

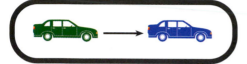

Mark one answer

- ⓐ a two-second time gap
- ⓑ one car length
- ⓒ 2 metres (6 feet 6 inches)
- ⓓ two car lengths

Question 25

Your overall stopping distance will be much longer when travelling

Mark one answer

- ⓐ in the rain
- ⓑ in fog
- ⓒ at night
- ⓓ in strong winds

Question 26

On a wet road what is the safest way to stop?

Mark one answer

- ⓐ Change gear without braking
- ⓑ Use the back brake only
- ⓒ Use the front brake only
- ⓓ Use both brakes

Question 27

The road surface is very important to motorcyclists because

Mark one answer

- ⓐ there can be many areas where road markings are poor
- ⓑ some roads are tarmac and others concrete
- ⓒ as traffic increases there is less room for riders
- ⓓ only a small part of the tyre touches the road

Question 28

Road surface is very important to motorcyclists. Which FOUR of these are more likely to reduce the stability of your machine?

Mark four answers

- ⓐ Potholes
- ⓑ Drain covers
- ⓒ Concrete
- ⓓ Oil patches
- ⓔ Tarmac
- ⓕ Loose gravel

Question 29

You are riding in town at night. The roads are wet after rain. The reflections from wet surfaces will

Mark one answer

- a affect your stopping distance
- b affect your road holding
- c make it easy to see unlit objects
- d make it hard to see unlit objects

Question 30

What is the most common cause of skidding?

Mark one answer

- a Worn tyres
- b Driver error
- c Other vehicles
- d Pedestrians

Question 31

You are driving in heavy rain. Your steering suddenly becomes very light. You should

Mark one answer

- a steer towards the side of the road
- b apply gentle acceleration
- c brake firmly to reduce speed
- d ease off the accelerator

Question 32

You are riding in heavy rain when your rear wheel skids as you accelerate. To get control again you must

Mark one answer

- a change down to a lower gear
- b ease off the throttle
- c brake to reduce speed
- d put your feet down

Question 33

You have driven through a flood. What is the first thing you should do?

Mark one answer

- a Stop and check the tyres
- b Stop and dry the brakes
- c Check your exhaust
- d Test your brakes

Question 34

You are driving along a country road. You see this sign. AFTER dealing safely with the hazard you should always

Mark one answer

- a check your tyre pressures
- b switch on your hazard warning lights
- c accelerate briskly
- d test your brakes

Question 35

Braking distances on ice can be

Mark one answer

- ⓐ twice the normal distance
- ⓑ five times the normal distance
- ⓒ seven times the normal distance
- ⓓ ten times the normal distance

Question 36

Freezing conditions will affect the distance it takes you to come to a stop. You should expect stopping distances to increase by up to

Mark one answer

- ⓐ two times
- ⓑ three times
- ⓒ five times
- ⓓ ten times

Question 37

You are driving on an icy road. How can you avoid wheelspin?

Mark one answer

- ⓐ Drive at a slow speed in as high a gear as possible
- ⓑ Use the handbrake if the wheels start to slip
- ⓒ Brake gently and repeatedly
- ⓓ Drive in a low gear at all times

Question 38

Skidding is mainly caused by

Mark one answer

- ⓐ the weather
- ⓑ the driver
- ⓒ the vehicle
- ⓓ the road

Question 39

It is snowing. Before starting your journey you should

Mark one answer

- ⓐ think if you need to ride at all
- ⓑ try to avoid taking a passenger
- ⓒ plan a route avoiding towns
- ⓓ take a hot drink before setting out

Question 40

You are driving in freezing conditions. What should you do when approaching a sharp bend?

Mark two answers

- ⓐ Slow down before you reach the bend
- ⓑ Gently apply your handbrake
- ⓒ Firmly use your footbrake
- ⓓ Coast into the bend
- ⓔ Avoid sudden steering movements

Question 41

When riding in extremely cold conditions what can you do to keep warm?

Mark one answer

ⓐ Stay close to the vehicles in front
ⓑ Wear suitable clothing
ⓒ Lie flat on the tank
ⓓ Put one hand on the exhaust pipe

Question 42

You are turning left on a slippery road. The back of your vehicle slides to the right. You should

Mark one answer

ⓐ brake firmly and not turn the steering wheel
ⓑ steer carefully to the left
ⓒ steer carefully to the right
ⓓ brake firmly and steer to the left

Question 43

You are braking on a wet road. Your vehicle begins to skid. Your vehicle does not have anti-lock brakes. What is the FIRST thing you should do?

Mark one answer

ⓐ Quickly pull up the handbrake
ⓑ Release the footbrake fully
ⓒ Push harder on the brake pedal
ⓓ Gently use the accelerator

Question 44

How can you tell when you are driving over black ice?

Mark one answer

ⓐ It is easier to brake
ⓑ The noise from your tyres sounds louder
ⓒ You see black ice on the road
ⓓ Your steering feels light

Question 45

Coasting the vehicle

Mark one answer

ⓐ improves the driver's control
ⓑ makes steering easier
ⓒ reduces the driver's control
ⓓ uses more fuel

Question 46

Before starting a journey in freezing weather you should clear ice and snow from your vehicle's

Mark four answers

ⓐ aerial
ⓑ windows
ⓒ bumper
ⓓ lights
ⓔ mirrors
ⓕ number plates

Question 47

You are driving in falling snow. Your wipers are not clearing the windscreen. You should

Mark one answer

- ⓐ set the windscreen demister to cool
- ⓑ be prepared to clear the windscreen by hand
- ⓒ use the windscreen washers
- ⓓ partly open the front windows

Question 48

You are trying to move off on snow. You should use

Mark one answer

- ⓐ the lowest gear you can
- ⓑ the highest gear you can
- ⓒ a high engine speed
- ⓓ the handbrake and footbrake together

Question 49

When driving in falling snow you should

Mark one answer

- ⓐ brake firmly and quickly
- ⓑ be ready to steer sharply
- ⓒ use sidelights only
- ⓓ brake gently in plenty of time

Question 50

The MAIN benefit of having four-wheel drive is to improve

Mark one answer

- ⓐ road holding
- ⓑ fuel consumption
- ⓒ stopping distances
- ⓓ passenger comfort

Question 51

When driving in fog in daylight you should use

Mark one answer

- ⓐ sidelights
- ⓑ full beam headlights
- ⓒ hazard lights
- ⓓ dipped headlights

Question 52

Why should you ride with a dipped headlight on in the daytime?

Mark one answer

- ⓐ It helps other road users to see you
- ⓑ It means that you can ride faster
- ⓒ Other vehicles will get out of the way
- ⓓ So that it is already on when it gets dark

Question 53

Motorcyclists are only allowed to use high-intensity rear fog lights when

Mark one answer

- a) a pillion passenger is being carried
- b) they ride a large touring machine
- c) visibility is 100 metres (328 feet) or less
- d) they are riding on the road for the first time

Question 54

In very hot weather the road surface can get soft. Which TWO of the following will be affected most?

Mark two answers

- a) The suspension
- b) The steering
- c) The braking
- d) The exhaust

Question 55

In very hot weather the road surface can get soft. Which TWO of the following will be affected most?

Mark two answers

- a) The suspension
- b) The grip of the tyres
- c) The braking
- d) The exhaust

Question 56

You are riding in very hot weather. What are TWO effects that melting tar has on the control of your machine?

Mark two answers

- a) It can make the surface slippery
- b) It can reduce tyre grip
- c) It can reduce stopping distances
- d) It can improve braking efficiency

Question 57

Where are you most likely to be affected by a sidewind?

Mark one answer

- a) On a narrow country lane
- b) On an open stretch of road
- c) On a busy stretch of road
- d) On a long, straight road

Question 58

In windy conditions you need to take extra care when

Mark one answer

- a) using the brakes
- b) making a hill start
- c) turning into a narrow road
- d) passing pedal cyclists

Question 59

Your indicators may be difficult to see in bright sunlight. What should you do?

Mark one answer

- (a) Put your indicator on earlier
- (b) Give an arm signal as well as using your indicator
- (c) Touch the brake several times to show the stop lights
- (d) Turn as quickly as you can

Question 60

You are riding at night. To be seen more easily you should

Mark two answers

- (a) ride with your headlight on dipped beam
- (b) wear reflective clothing
- (c) keep the motorcycle clean
- (d) stay well out to the right
- (e) wear waterproof clothing

Question 61

When riding at night you should

Mark two answers

- (a) ride with your headlight on dipped beam
- (b) wear reflective clothing
- (c) wear a tinted visor
- (d) ride in the centre of the road
- (e) give arm signals

Question 62

You MUST use your headlight

Mark three answers

- (a) when riding in a group
- (b) at night when street lighting is poor
- (c) when carrying a passenger
- (d) on motorways during darkness
- (e) at times of poor visibility
- (f) when parked on an unlit road

Question 63

You are about to go down a steep hill. To control the speed of your vehicle you should

Mark one answer

- (a) select a high gear and use the brakes carefully
- (b) select a high gear and use the brakes firmly
- (c) select a low gear and use the brakes carefully
- (d) select a low gear and avoid using the brakes

Question 64

You are on a long, downhill slope. What should you do to help control the speed of your vehicle?

Mark one answer

- (a) Select neutral
- (b) Select a lower gear
- (c) Grip the handbrake firmly
- (d) Apply the parking brake gently

Question 65

How can you use the engine of your vehicle as a brake?

Mark one answer

- a By changing to a lower gear
- b By selecting reverse gear
- c By changing to a higher gear
- d By selecting neutral gear

Question 66

You wish to park facing DOWNHILL. Which TWO of the following should you do?

Mark two answers

- a Turn the steering wheel towards the kerb
- b Park close to the bumper of another car
- c Park with two wheels on the kerb
- d Put the handbrake on firmly
- e Turn the steering wheel away from the kerb

Question 67

You are driving in a built-up area. You approach a speed hump. You should

Mark one answer

- a move across to the left-hand side of the road
- b wait for any pedestrians to cross
- c slow your vehicle right down
- d stop and check both pavements

Question 68

When approaching a right-hand bend you should keep well to the left. Why is this?

Mark one answer

- a To improve your view of the road
- b To overcome the effect of the road's slope
- c To let faster traffic from behind overtake
- d To be positioned safely if the vehicle skids

Question 69

You should not overtake when

Mark three answers

- a intending to turn left shortly afterwards
- b in a one-way street
- c approaching a junction
- d driving up a long hill
- e the view ahead is blocked

Question 70

You are riding through a flood. Which TWO should you do?

Mark two answers

- a) Keep in a high gear and stand up on the footrests
- b) Keep the engine running fast to keep water out of the exhaust
- c) Ride slowly and test your brakes when you are out of the water
- d) Turn your headlight off to avoid any electrical damage

Question 71

You have just ridden through a flood. When clear of the water you should test your

Mark one answer

- a) starter motor
- b) headlight
- c) steering
- d) brakes

Question 72

When going through flood water you should ride

Mark one answer

- a) quickly in a high gear
- b) slowly in a high gear
- c) quickly in a low gear
- d) slowly in a low gear

Question 73

You have to ride in foggy weather. You should

Mark two answers

- a) stay close to the centre of the road
- b) switch only your sidelights on
- c) switch on your dipped headlights
- d) be aware of others not using their headlights
- e) always ride in the gutter to see the kerb

Question 74

When riding at night you should NOT

Mark one answer

- a) switch on full beam headlights
- b) overtake slower vehicles in front
- c) use dipped beam headlights
- d) use tinted glasses, lenses or visors

Question 75

At a mini roundabout it is important that a motorcyclist should avoid

Mark one answer

- a) turning right
- b) using signals
- c) taking lifesavers
- d) the painted area

Question 76

Which of the following should you do when riding in fog?

Mark two answers

a) Keep close to the vehicle in front
b) Use your dipped headlight
c) Ride close to the centre of the road
d) Keep your visor or goggles clear
e) Keep the vehicle in front in view

Question 77

You are riding on a motorway in a crosswind. You should take extra care when

Mark two answers

a) approaching service areas
b) overtaking a large vehicle
c) riding in slow-moving traffic
d) approaching an exit
e) riding in exposed places

Question 78

The roads are icy. You should drive slowly

Mark one answer

a) in the highest gear possible
b) in the lowest gear possible
c) with the handbrake partly on
d) with your left foot on the brake

Question 79

You are driving along a wet road. How can you tell if your vehicle is aquaplaning?

Mark one answer

a) The engine will stall
b) The engine noise will increase
c) The steering will feel very heavy
d) The steering will feel very light

Question 80

You have just gone through deep water. To dry off the brakes you should

Mark one answer

a) accelerate and keep to a high speed for a short time
b) drive or ride slowly while pressing the brake pedal
c) avoid using the brakes at all for a few miles
d) stop for at least an hour to allow them time to dry

Question 81

How can you tell if you are driving on ice?

Mark two answers

a) The tyres make a rumbling noise
b) The tyres make hardly any noise
c) The steering becomes heavier
d) The steering becomes lighter

Answers and explanations

Q001 b

Q002 b

Q003 d

Q004 c You should brake rapidly and firmly.

Q005 b,c

Q006 b

Q007 c

Q008 b A vehicle fitted with anti-lock brakes is very difficult, but not impossible, to skid. Take care if the road surface is loose or wet.

Q009 b,c

Q010 c

Q011 c

Q012 c

Q013 b

Q014 b

Q015 b

Q016 a Note this is the braking distance. The overall stopping distance is further because you have to add 'thinking' distance.

Q017 c Remember, therefore, to allow a bigger gap when following another vehicle.

Q018 d

Q019 d

Q020 b

Q021 c

Q022 a,c,e

Q023 b

Q024 a

Q025 a

Q026 d

Q027 d

Q028 a,b,d,f

Q029 d

Q030 b

Q031 d This problem is sometimes called aquaplaning. Your tyres build up a thin film of water between them and the road and lose all grip. The steering suddenly feels light and probably uncontrollable. The solution is to ease off the accelerator until you feel the tyres grip the road again.

Q032 b

Q033 d Your brakes may be wet. The first thing you should do is check them and then dry them.

Q034 d Drive slowly forwards with your left foot gently on the footbrake. This helps dry out the brakes.

Q035 d

Q036 d

Q037 a

Q038 b Skidding is usually caused by harsh braking, harsh acceleration or harsh steering – all actions of the driver. You are, however, more likely to cause a skid in a poorly maintained car, in bad weather or on a poor road surface.

Q039 a

Q040 a,e Braking on an icy bend is extremely dangerous. It could cause your vehicle to spin.

Q041 b

Q042 c

Q043 b Note that the question asks for the first thing you should do, which is always to remove the cause of the skid – in this case braking. You would next need to re-apply the brakes more gently. 'c' is wrong because braking harder would increase the skid.

Q044 d Black ice is normally invisible when you are driving. The tyres will lose grip with the road which will make the steering feel light.

Q045 c Coasting means driving along with the clutch pedal down. This disconnects the engine and gears from the drive wheels of the car, so you have less control.

Q046 b,d,e,f

Q047 b Bear in mind that you would have to stop first.

Q048 b A higher gear helps avoid wheelspin.

Q049 d

Q050 a

Q051 d Sidelights are not enough so 'a' is wrong. Full beam headlights tend to reflect back the fog, so 'b' is also incorrect.

Q052 a Motorcycles are small and difficult to see. Anything that increases your chances of being seen by other road users is a good thing.

Q053 c

Q054 b,c

Q055 b,c

Q056 a,b

Q057 b

Q058 d In windy conditions cyclists are all too easily blown about and may wobble or steer off course.

Answers and explanations

Q059	b
Q060	a,b
Q061	a,b
Q062	b,d,e
Q063	c A low gear will help control your speed, but on a steep hill you will also need your brakes.
Q064	b You should ideally have selected the lower gear before starting down the slope. 'a' would be likely to make your car go faster as you would no longer be in any gear at all.
Q065	a
Q066	a,d If the handbrake should fail, the car will roll into the kerb and not down the road.

Q067	c
Q068	a You can see further round the bend earlier if you keep to the left.
Q069	a,c,e
Q070	b,c
Q071	d
Q072	d
Q073	c,d
Q074	d
Q075	d
Q076	b,d
Q077	b,e
Q078	a
Q079	d
Q080	b
Q081	b,d

Driving Theory
Test
Questions
2000/2001

Hazard Awareness

We won't fail you

Question 1

You see this sign on the rear of a slow-moving lorry that you want to pass. It is travelling in the middle lane of a three lane motorway. You should

Mark one answer

- a cautiously approach the lorry then pass on either side
- b follow the lorry until you can leave the motorway
- c wait on the hard shoulder until the lorry has stopped
- d approach with care and keep to the left of the lorry

Question 2

Where would you expect to see these markers?

Mark two answers

- a On a motorway sign
- b At the entrance to a narrow bridge
- c On a large goods vehicle
- d On a builder's skip placed on the road

Question 3

What does this signal from a police officer mean to oncoming traffic?

Mark one answer

- a Go ahead
- b Stop
- c Turn left
- d Turn right

Question 4

What is the main hazard shown in this picture?

Mark one answer

- a Vehicles turning right
- b Vehicles doing U-turns
- c The cyclist crossing the road
- d Parked cars around the corner

Question 5

Which road user has caused a hazard?

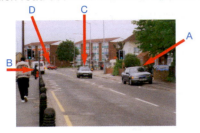

Mark one answer

- ⓐ The parked car (arrowed A)
- ⓑ The pedestrian waiting to cross (arrowed B)
- ⓒ The moving car (arrowed C)
- ⓓ The car turning (arrowed D)

Question 6

What should the driver of the car approaching the crossing do?

Mark one answer

- ⓐ Continue at the same speed
- ⓑ Sound the horn
- ⓒ Drive through quickly
- ⓓ Slow down and get ready to stop

Question 7

What should the driver of the red car do?

Mark one answer

- ⓐ Wave the pedestrians who are waiting to cross
- ⓑ Wait for the pedestrian in the road to cross
- ⓒ Quickly drive behind the pedestrian in the road
- ⓓ Tell the pedestrian in the road she should not have crossed

Question 8

What THREE things should the driver of the grey car (arrowed) be especially aware of?

Mark three answers

- ⓐ Pedestrians stepping out between cars
- ⓑ Other cars behind the grey car
- ⓒ Doors opening on parked cars
- ⓓ The bumpy road surface
- ⓔ Cars leaving parking spaces
- ⓕ Empty parking spaces

Question 9

What should the driver of the red car (arrowed) do?

Mark one answer

- a) Sound the horn to tell other drivers where he is
- b) Squeeze through the gap
- c) Wave the driver of the white car to go on
- d) Wait until the car blocking the way has moved

Question 10

What should the driver of the grey car (arrowed) do?

Mark one answer

- a) Cross if the way is clear
- b) Reverse out of the box junction
- c) Wait in the same place until the lights are green
- d) Wait until the lights are red then cross

Question 11

The red lights are flashing. What should you do when coming up to this level crossing?

Mark one answer

- a) Go through quickly
- b) Go through carefully
- c) Stop before the barrier
- d) Switch on hazard warning lights

Question 12

What are TWO main hazards you should be aware of when going along this street?

Mark two answers

- a) Glare from the sun
- b) Car doors opening suddenly
- c) Lack of road markings
- d) The headlights on parked cars being switched on
- e) Large goods vehicles
- f) Children running out from between vehicles

Question 13

What is the main hazard you should be aware of when following this cyclist?

Mark one answer

ⓐ The cyclist may move into the left and dismount

ⓑ The cyclist may swerve out into the road

ⓒ The contents of the cyclist's carrier may fall onto the road

ⓓ The cyclist may wish to turn right at the end of the road

Question 14

The driver of which car has caused a hazard?

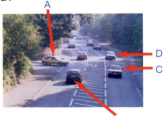

Mark one answer

ⓐ Car A

ⓑ Car B

ⓒ Car C

ⓓ Car D

Question 15

You think the driver of the vehicle in front has forgotten to cancel the right indicator. You should

Mark one answer

ⓐ flash your lights to alert the driver

ⓑ sound your horn before overtaking

ⓒ overtake on the left if there is room

ⓓ stay behind and not overtake

Question 16

What is the main hazard the driver of the red car (arrowed) should be most aware of?

Mark one answer

ⓐ Glare from the sun may affect the driver's vision

ⓑ The black car may stop suddenly

ⓒ The bus may move out into the road

ⓓ Oncoming vehicles will assume the driver is turning right

Question 17

In heavy motorway traffic you are being followed closely by the vehicle behind. How can you lower the risk of an accident?

Mark one answer

- [a] Increase your distance from the vehicle in front
- [b] Tap your foot on the brake pedal sharply
- [c] Switch on your hazard lights
- [d] Move onto the hard shoulder and stop

Question 18

You are travelling on this dual carriageway. Why may you need to slow down?

Mark one answer

- [a] There is a broken white line in the centre
- [b] There are solid white lines either side
- [c] There are roadworks ahead of you
- [d] There are no footpaths

Question 19

What does the solid white line at the side of the road indicate?

Mark one answer

- [a] Traffic lights ahead
- [b] Edge of the carriageway
- [c] Footpath on the left
- [d] Cycle path

Question 20

You see this sign ahead. You should expect the road to

Mark one answer

- [a] go steeply uphill
- [b] go steeply downhill
- [c] bend sharply to the left
- [d] bend sharply to the right

Question 21

You are approaching this cyclist. You should

Mark one answer

- ⓐ overtake before the cyclist gets to the junction
- ⓑ flash your headlights at the cyclist
- ⓒ slow down and allow the cyclist to turn
- ⓓ overtake the cyclist on the left-hand side

Question 22

You have just been overtaken by this motorcyclist who is cutting in sharply. You should

Mark one answer

- ⓐ sound the horn
- ⓑ brake firmly
- ⓒ keep a safe gap
- ⓓ flash your lights

Question 23

Why must you take extra care when turning right at this junction?

Mark one answer

- ⓐ Road surface is poor
- ⓑ Footpaths are narrow
- ⓒ Road markings are faint
- ⓓ There is reduced visibility

Question 24

What is the main hazard in this picture?

Mark one answer

- ⓐ The pedestrian
- ⓑ The parked cars
- ⓒ The junction on the left
- ⓓ The driveway on the left

Question 25

This yellow sign on a vehicle indicates this is

Mark one answer

ⓐ a vehicle broken down
ⓑ a school bus
ⓒ an ice cream van
ⓓ a private ambulance

Question 26

You are driving towards this level crossing. What would be the first warning of an approaching train?

Mark one answer

ⓐ Both half barriers down
ⓑ A steady amber light
ⓒ One half barrier down
ⓓ Twin flashing red lights

Question 27

You are driving along this motorway. It is raining. When following this lorry you should

Mark two answers

ⓐ allow at least a two-second gap
ⓑ move left and drive on the hard shoulder
ⓒ allow at least a four-second gap
ⓓ be aware of spray reducing your vision
ⓔ move right and stay in the right-hand lane

Question 28

You are behind this cyclist. When the traffic lights change, what should you do?

Mark one answer

ⓐ Try to move off before the cyclist
ⓑ Allow the cyclist time and room
ⓒ Turn right but give the cyclist room
ⓓ Tap your horn and drive through first

Question 29

You are driving towards this left-hand bend. What dangers should you be aware of?

Mark one answer

- ⓐ A vehicle overtaking you
- ⓑ No white lines in the centre of the road
- ⓒ No sign to warn you of the bend
- ⓓ Pedestrians walking towards you

Question 30

When approaching this bridge you should give way to

Mark one answer

- ⓐ bicycles
- ⓑ buses
- ⓒ motorcycles
- ⓓ cars

Question 31

What type of vehicle could you expect to meet in the middle of the road?

Mark one answer

- ⓐ Lorry
- ⓑ Bicycle
- ⓒ Car
- ⓓ Motorcycle

Question 32

When approaching this hazard why should you slow down?

Mark two answers

- ⓐ Because of the bend
- ⓑ Because it's hard to see to the right
- ⓒ Because of approaching traffic
- ⓓ Because of animals crossing
- ⓔ Because of the level crossing

Question 33

While driving, you see this sign ahead. You should

Mark one answer

- a stop at the sign
- b slow, but continue around the bend
- c slow to a crawl and continue
- d stop and look for open farm gates

Question 34

Why should the junction on the left be kept clear?

Mark one answer

- a To allow vehicles to enter and emerge
- b To allow the bus to reverse
- c To allow vehicles to make a 'U' turn
- d To allow vehicles to park

Question 35

When the traffic lights change to green the white car should

Mark one answer

- a wait for the cyclist to pull away
- b move off quickly and turn in front of the cyclist
- c move close up to the cyclist to beat the lights
- d sound the horn to warn the cyclist

Question 36

You intend to turn left at the traffic lights. Just before turning you should

Mark one answer

- a check your right mirror
- b move close up to the white car
- c straddle the lanes
- d check for bicycles on your left

Question 37

You should reduce your speed when driving along this road because

Mark one answer

- a there is a staggered junction ahead
- b there is a low bridge ahead
- c there is a change in the road surface
- d the road ahead narrows

Question 38

You are driving at 60 mph. As you approach this hazard you should

Mark one answer

- a maintain your speed
- b reduce your speed
- c take the next right turn
- d take the next left turn

Question 39

The traffic ahead of you in the left lane is slowing. You should

Mark two answers

- a be wary of cars on your right cutting in
- b accelerate past the vehicles in the left lane
- c pull up on the left-hand verge
- d move across and continue in the right-hand lane
- e slow down keeping a safe separation distance

Question 40

What might you expect to happen in this situation?

Mark one answer

- a Traffic will move into the right-hand lane
- b Traffic speed will increase
- c Traffic will move into the left-hand lane
- d Traffic will not need to change position

Question 41

You are driving on a road with several lanes. You see these signs above the lanes. What do they mean?

Mark one answer

- a The two right lanes are open
- b The two left lanes are open
- c Traffic in the left lanes should stop
- d Traffic in the right lanes should stop

Question 42

At this blind junction you must stop

Mark one answer

- a behind the line, then edge forward to see clearly
- b beyond the line at a point where you can see clearly
- c only if there is traffic on the main road
- d only if you are turning to the right

Question 43

As a provisional licence holder, you must not drive a motor car

Mark two answers

- a at more than 50 mph
- b on your own
- c on the motorway
- d under the age of 18 years of age at night
- e with passengers in the rear seats

Question 44

To drive or ride you MUST be able to read a number plate from what distance?

Mark one answer

- a 10 metres (32 feet)
- b 15 metres (50 feet)
- c 20.5 metres (67 feet)
- d 25.5 metres (84 feet)

Question 45

You are about to travel home. You cannot find the glasses you need to wear. You should

Mark one answer

- a go home slowly, keeping to quiet roads
- b borrow a friend's glasses and use those
- c go home at night, so that the lights will help you
- d find a way of getting home without driving or riding

Question 46

You MUST wear glasses or contact lenses when driving on public roads if

Mark one answer

- ⓐ you are the holder of an orange badge
- ⓑ you cannot read a vehicle number plate from a distance of 36 metres (120 feet) without them
- ⓒ there is an eyesight problem in your family
- ⓓ you cannot read a vehicle number plate from a distance of 20.5 metres (67 feet) without them

Question 47

As a driver you find that your eyesight has become very poor. Your optician says he cannot help you. The law says that you should tell

Mark one answer

- ⓐ the licensing authority
- ⓑ your own doctor
- ⓒ the local police station
- ⓓ another optician

Question 48

You find that you need glasses to read vehicle number plates at the required distance. When MUST you wear them?

Mark one answer

- ⓐ Only in bad weather conditions
- ⓑ At all times when driving or riding
- ⓒ Only when you think it necessary
- ⓓ Only in bad light or at night time

Question 49

After passing your driving test, you suffer from ill health. This affects your driving. You MUST

Mark one answer

- ⓐ inform your local police station
- ⓑ get on as best you can
- ⓒ not inform anyone as you hold a full licence
- ⓓ inform the licensing authority

Question 50

Which THREE result from drinking alcohol?

Mark three answers

- ⓐ Less control
- ⓑ A false sense of confidence
- ⓒ Faster reactions
- ⓓ Poor judgement of speed
- ⓔ Greater awareness of danger

Question 51

Which THREE of these are likely effects of drinking alcohol?

Mark three answers

- ⓐ Reduced co-ordination
- ⓑ Increased confidence
- ⓒ Poor judgement
- ⓓ Increased concentration
- ⓔ Faster reactions
- ⓕ Colour blindness

Question 52

Drinking any amount of alcohol is likely to

Mark three answers

ⓐ slow down your reactions to hazards

ⓑ increase the speed of your reactions

ⓒ worsen your judgement of speed

ⓓ improve your awareness of danger

ⓔ give a false sense of confidence

Question 53

You are invited to a pub lunch. You know that you will have to drive in the evening. What is your best course of action?

Mark one answer

ⓐ Avoid mixing your alcoholic drinks

ⓑ Not drink any alcohol at all

ⓒ Have some milk before drinking alcohol

ⓓ Eat a hot meal with your alcoholic drinks

Question 54

What else can seriously affect your concentration, other than alcoholic drinks?

Mark three answers

ⓐ Drugs

ⓑ Tiredness

ⓒ Tinted windows

ⓓ Contact lenses

ⓔ Loud music

Question 55

How does alcohol affect you?

Mark one answer

ⓐ It speeds up your reactions

ⓑ It increases your awareness

ⓒ It improves your co-ordination

ⓓ It reduces your concentration

Question 56

You have been convicted of driving whilst unfit through drink or drugs. You will find this is likely to cause the cost of one of the following to rise considerably. Which one?

Mark one answer

ⓐ Road fund licence

ⓑ Insurance premiums

ⓒ Vehicle test certificate

ⓓ Driving licence

Question 57

What advice should you give to a driver who has had a few alcoholic drinks at a party?

Mark one answer

ⓐ Have a strong cup of coffee and then drive home

ⓑ Drive home carefully and slowly

ⓒ Go home by public transport

ⓓ Wait a short while and then drive home

Question 58

You go to a social event and need to drive a short time after. What precaution should you take?

Mark one answer

ⓐ Avoid drinking alcohol on an empty stomach

ⓑ Drink plenty of coffee after drinking alcohol

ⓒ Avoid drinking alcohol completely

ⓓ Drink plenty of milk before drinking alcohol

Question 59

Your doctor has given you a course of medicine. Why should you ask how it will affect you?

Mark one answer

ⓐ Drugs make you a better driver or rider by quickening your reactions

ⓑ You will have to let your insurance company know about the medicine

ⓒ Some types of medicine can cause your reactions to slow down

ⓓ The medicine you take may affect your hearing

Question 60

You have been taking medicine for a few days which made you feel drowsy. Today you feel better but still need to take the medicine. You should only drive

Mark one answer

ⓐ if your journey is necessary

ⓑ at night on quiet roads

ⓒ if someone goes with you

ⓓ after checking with your doctor

Question 61

You are about to return home from holiday when you become ill. A doctor prescribes drugs which are likely to affect your driving. You should

Mark one answer

ⓐ drive only if someone is with you

ⓑ avoid driving on motorways

ⓒ not drive yourself

ⓓ never drive at more than 30 mph

Question 62

During periods of illness your ability to drive may be impaired. You MUST

Mark two answers

ⓐ see your doctor each time before you drive

ⓑ only take smaller doses of any medicines

ⓒ be medically fit to drive

ⓓ not drive after taking certain medicines

ⓔ take all your medicines with you when you drive

Question 63

You are not sure if your cough medicine will affect you. What TWO things could you do?

Mark two answers

ⓐ Ask your doctor
ⓑ Check the medicine label
ⓒ Drive or ride if you feel alright
ⓓ Ask a friend or relative for advice

Question 64

You take some cough medicine given to you by a friend. What should you do before driving?

Mark one answer

ⓐ Ask your friend if taking the medicine affected their driving
ⓑ Drink some strong coffee one hour before driving
ⓒ Check the label to see if the medicine will affect your driving
ⓓ Drive a short distance to see if the medicine is affecting your driving

Question 65

You feel drowsy when driving. You should

Mark two answers

ⓐ stop and rest as soon as possible
ⓑ turn the heater up to keep you warm and comfortable
ⓒ make sure you have a good supply of fresh air
ⓓ continue with your journey but drive more slowly
ⓔ close the car windows to help you concentrate

Question 66

You are driving along a motorway and become tired. You should

Mark two answers

ⓐ stop at the next service area and rest
ⓑ leave the motorway at the next exit and rest
ⓒ increase your speed and turn up the radio volume
ⓓ close all your windows and set heating to warm
ⓔ pull up on the hard shoulder and change drivers

Question 67

You are taking drugs that are likely to affect your driving. What should you do?

Mark one answer

- a) Seek medical advice before driving
- b) Limit your driving to essential journeys
- c) Only drive if accompanied by a full licence-holder
- d) Drive only for short distances

Question 68

You are about to drive home. You feel very tired and have a severe headache. You should

Mark one answer

- a) wait until you are fit and well before driving
- b) drive home, but take a tablet for headaches
- c) drive home if you can stay awake for the journey
- d) wait for a short time, then drive home slowly

Question 69

If you are feeling tired it is best to stop as soon as you can. Until then you should

Mark one answer

- a) increase your speed to find a stopping place quickly
- b) ensure a supply of fresh air
- c) gently tap the steering wheel
- d) keep changing speed to improve concentration

Question 70

You are on a motorway. You feel tired. You should

Mark one answer

- a) carry on but go slowly
- b) leave the motorway at the next exit
- c) complete your journey as quickly as possible
- d) stop on the hard shoulder

Question 71

If your motorway journey seems boring and you feel drowsy whilst driving you should

Mark one answer

- a) open a window and drive to the next service area
- b) stop on the hard shoulder for a sleep
- c) speed up to arrive at your destination sooner
- d) slow down and let other drivers overtake

Question 72

You are planning a long journey. Do you need to plan rest stops?

Mark one answer

(a) Yes, you should plan to stop every half an hour

(b) Yes, regular stops help concentration

(c) No, you will be less tired if you get there as soon as possible

(d) No, only fuel stops will be needed

Question 73

Driving long distances can be tiring. You can prevent this by

Mark three answers

(a) stopping every so often for a walk

(b) opening a window for some fresh air

(c) ensuring plenty of refreshment breaks

(d) completing the journey without stopping

(e) eating a large meal before driving

Question 74

Which TWO things would help to keep you alert during a long journey?

Mark two answers

(a) Finishing your journey as fast as you can

(b) Keeping off the motorways and using country roads

(c) Making sure that you get plenty of fresh air

(d) Making regular stops for refreshments

Question 75

Which THREE are likely to make you lose concentration while driving?

Mark three answers

(a) Looking at road maps

(b) Listening to loud music

(c) Using your windscreen washers

(d) Looking in your wing mirror

(e) Using a mobile phone

Question 76

You get cold and wet when riding. Which TWO are likely to happen?

Mark two answers

(a) You may lose concentration

(b) You may slide off the seat

(c) Your visor may freeze up

(d) Your reaction times may be slower

(e) Your helmet may loosen

Question 77

A driver pulls out of a side road in front of you. You have to brake hard.
You should

Mark one answer

(a) ignore the error and stay calm

(b) flash your lights to show your annoyance

(c) sound your horn to show your annoyance

(d) overtake as soon as possible

Question 78

Another driver does something that upsets you. You should

Mark one answer

- ⓐ try not to react
- ⓑ let them know how you feel
- ⓒ flash your headlights several times
- ⓓ sound your horn

Question 79

Another driver's behaviour has upset you. It may help if you

Mark one answer

- ⓐ stop and take a break
- ⓑ shout abusive language
- ⓒ gesture to them with your hand
- ⓓ follow their car, flashing the headlights

Question 80

An elderly person's driving ability could be affected because they may be unable to

Mark one answer

- ⓐ obtain car insurance
- ⓑ understand road signs
- ⓒ react very quickly
- ⓓ give signals correctly

Question 81

You take the wrong route and find you are on a one-way street. You should

Mark one answer

- ⓐ reverse out of the road
- ⓑ turn round in a side road
- ⓒ continue to the end of the road
- ⓓ reverse into a driveway

Question 82

Why should you check over your shoulder before turning right into a side road?

Mark one answer

- ⓐ To make sure the road is clear
- ⓑ To check for emerging traffic
- ⓒ To check for overtaking vehicles
- ⓓ To confirm your intention to turn

Question 83

What could happen if you do not keep to the left on right-hand bends?

Mark one answer

a) You may not be able to see overtaking vehicles

b) You may not be able to judge the sharpness of the bend

c) Your head may cross over the centre line

d) You may not be able to see vehicles to the rear

Question 84

You are riding up to a zebra crossing. You intend to stop for waiting pedestrians. How could you let them know you are stopping?

Mark one answer

a) By signalling with your left arm

b) By waving them across

c) By flashing your headlight

d) By signalling with your right arm

Question 85

You have just passed these warning lights. What hazard would you expect to see next?

Mark one answer

a) A level crossing with no barrier

b) An ambulance station

c) A school crossing patrol

d) An opening bridge

Question 86

You are driving along this road. The driver on the left is reversing from a driveway. You should

Mark one answer

a) move to the opposite side of the road

b) drive through as you have priority

c) sound your horn and be prepared to stop

d) speed up and drive through quickly

Question 87

Which of the following types of glasses should not be worn when driving or riding at night?

Mark one answer

ⓐ Half-moon
ⓑ Round
ⓒ Bi-focal
ⓓ Tinted

Question 88

Why should you be especially cautious when going past this bus?

Mark two answers

ⓐ There is traffic approaching in the distance
ⓑ The driver may open the door
ⓒ It may suddenly move off
ⓓ People may cross the road in front of it
ⓔ There are bicycles parked on the pavement

Question 89

You have been involved in an argument before starting your journey. This has made you feel angry. You should

Mark one answer

ⓐ start to drive, but open a window
ⓑ drive slower than normal and turn your radio on
ⓒ have an alcoholic drink to help you relax before driving
ⓓ calm down before you start to drive

Answers and explanations

Q001	d	
Q002	c,d	
Q003	b	
Q004	c	
Q005	a	
Q006	d	
Q007	b	
Q008	a,c,e	
Q009	d	
Q010	a	
Q011	c	
Q012	b,f	
Q013	b	
Q014	a	
Q015	d	
Q016	c	
Q017	a	
Q018	c	
Q019	b	
Q020	c	
Q021	c	
Q022	c	
Q023	d	
Q024	a	
Q025	b	
Q026	b	
Q027	c,d	
Q028	b	
Q029	d	
Q030	b	
Q031	a	
Q032	a,e	
Q033	b	

Q034 a

Q035 a

Q036 d

Q037 a

Q038 b

Q039 a,e

Q040 c

Q041 b

Q042 a

Q043 b,c

Q044 c Glasses or contact lenses may be worn.

Q045 d It is illegal to drive if you cannot satisfy the requirements of the eyesight test.

Q046 d

Q047 a You must not drive if your eyesight becomes so poor that you can no longer meet the minimum legal requirements, wearing glasses or contact lenses if necessary.

Q048 b If you need glasses to drive you must wear them whenever you are driving, so 'b' is correct.

Q049 d In the event of a short-term illness, like flu, that affected your ability to drive, you would simply not drive until you are recovered.

Q050 a,b,d

Q051 a,b,c

Answers and explanations

Q052 a,c,e

Q053 b

Q054 a,b,e

Q055 d You may well feel, after drinking, that 'a', 'b' and 'c' are true. However, this is never correct and makes you dangerous.

Q056 b

Q057 c The only sensible answer is don't drink and drive.

Q058 c

Q059 c

Q060 d

Q061 c

Q062 c,d

Q063 a,b

Q064 c

Q065 a,c

Q066 a,b

Q067 a A significant number of drugs, even those you can buy in the chemist, can affect your ability to drive. Sometimes a warning is given on the packet, but if in any doubt seek medical advice.

Q068 a

Q069 b

Q070 b If you feel tired you greatly increase your chances of having an accident. You must stop, but as you are on a motorway you cannot do this unless you leave at the next exit or find a service station before it.

Q071 a

Q072 b

Q073 a,b,c

Q074 c,d

Q075 a,b,e 'c' and 'd' are normal parts of the driving task.

Q076 a,d

Q077 a

Q078 a

Q079 a

Q080 c

Q081 c

Q082 c Overtaking vehicles might not be visible in your mirrors.

Q083 c As you bank over, your head might cross over to the other side of the road if you are too close to the centre line.

Q084 d

Q085 c

Q086 c

Q087 d

Q088 c,d

Q089 d

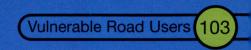
Driving Theory
Test
Questions

2000/2001

Vulnerable Road Users

Question 1

You should not ride too closely behind a lorry because

Mark one answer

ⓐ you will breathe in the lorry's exhaust fumes

ⓑ wind from the lorry will slow you down

ⓒ drivers behind you may not be able to see you

ⓓ it will reduce your view ahead

Question 2

You are riding in fast-flowing traffic. The vehicle behind is following too closely. You should

Mark one answer

ⓐ slow down gradually to increase the gap in front of you

ⓑ slow down as quickly as possible by braking

ⓒ accelerate to get away from the vehicle behind you

ⓓ apply the brakes sharply to warn the driver behind

Question 3

You are riding along a main road with many side roads. Why should you be particularly careful?

Mark one answer

ⓐ Gusts of wind from the side roads may push you off course

ⓑ Drivers coming out from side roads may not see you

ⓒ The road will be more slippery where cars have been turning

ⓓ Drivers will be travelling slowly when they approach a junction

Question 4

You are on a country road. What should you expect to see coming towards you on YOUR side of the road?

Mark one answer

ⓐ Motorcycles

ⓑ Bicycles

ⓒ Pedestrians

ⓓ Horse riders

Question 5

Which sign means that there may be people walking along the road?

Mark one answer

ⓐ

ⓑ

ⓒ

ⓓ

Question 6

You are turning left into a side road. Pedestrians are crossing the road near the junction. You must

Mark one answer

ⓐ wave them on

ⓑ sound your horn

ⓒ switch on your hazard lights

ⓓ wait for them to cross

Question 7

You are turning left at a junction. Pedestrians have started to cross the road. You should

Mark one answer

ⓐ go on, giving them plenty of room

ⓑ stop and wave at them to cross

ⓒ blow your horn and proceed

ⓓ give way to them

Question 8

You are turning left from a main road into a side road. People are already crossing the road into which you are turning. You should

Mark one answer

ⓐ continue, as it is your right of way

ⓑ signal to them to continue crossing

ⓒ wait and allow them to cross

ⓓ sound your horn to warn them of your presence

Question 9

You are at a road junction, turning into a minor road. There are pedestrians crossing the minor road. You should

Mark one answer

- ⓐ stop and wave the pedestrians across
- ⓑ sound your horn to let the pedestrians know that you are there
- ⓒ give way to the pedestrians who are already crossing
- ⓓ carry on; the pedestrians should give way to you

Question 10

You are turning left into a side road. What hazards should you be especially aware of?

Mark one answer

- ⓐ One-way street
- ⓑ Pedestrians
- ⓒ Traffic congestion
- ⓓ Parked vehicles

Question 11

You want to reverse into a side road. You are not sure that the area behind your car is clear. What should you do?

Mark one answer

- ⓐ Look through the rear window only
- ⓑ Get out and check
- ⓒ Check the mirrors only
- ⓓ Carry on, assuming it is clear

Question 12

You are about to reverse into a side road. A pedestrian wishes to cross behind you. You should

Mark one answer

- ⓐ wave to the pedestrian to stop
- ⓑ give way to the pedestrian
- ⓒ wave to the pedestrian to cross
- ⓓ reverse before the pedestrian starts to cross

Question 13

Who is especially in danger of not being seen as you reverse your car?

Mark one answer

- ⓐ Motorcyclists
- ⓑ Car drivers
- ⓒ Cyclists
- ⓓ Children

Question 14

You are reversing around a corner when you notice a pedestrian walking behind you. What should you do?

Mark one answer

ⓐ Slow down and wave the pedestrian across

ⓑ Continue reversing and steer round the pedestrian

ⓒ Stop and give way

ⓓ Continue reversing and sound your horn

Question 15

You intend to turn right into a side road. Just before turning you should check for motorcyclists who might be

Mark one answer

ⓐ overtaking on your left

ⓑ following you closely

ⓒ emerging from the side road

ⓓ overtaking on your right

Question 16

You want to turn right from a junction but your view is restricted by parked vehicles. What should you do?

Mark one answer

ⓐ Move out quickly, but be prepared to stop

ⓑ Sound your horn and pull out if there is no reply

ⓒ Stop, then move slowly forward until you have a clear view

ⓓ Stop, get out and look along the main road to check

Question 17

You are at the front of a queue of traffic waiting to turn right into a side road. Why is it important to check your right mirror just before turning?

Mark one answer

ⓐ To look for pedestrians about to cross

ⓑ To check for overtaking vehicles

ⓒ To make sure the side road is clear

ⓓ To check for emerging traffic

Question 18

In which THREE places would parking your vehicle cause danger or obstruction to other road users?

Mark three answers

ⓐ In front of a property entrance
ⓑ At or near a bus stop
ⓒ On your driveway
ⓓ In a marked parking space
ⓔ On the approach to a level crossing

Question 19

In which THREE places would parking cause an obstruction to others?

Mark three answers

ⓐ Near the brow of a hill
ⓑ In a lay-by
ⓒ Where the kerb is raised
ⓓ Where the kerb has been lowered for wheelchairs
ⓔ At or near a bus stop

Question 20

What must a driver do at a pelican crossing when the amber light is flashing?

Mark one answer

ⓐ Signal the pedestrian to cross
ⓑ Always wait for the green light before proceeding
ⓒ Give way to any pedestrians on the crossing
ⓓ Wait for the red-and-amber light before proceeding

Question 21

You have stopped at a pelican crossing. A disabled person is crossing slowly in front of you. The lights have now changed to green. You should

Mark two answers

ⓐ allow the person to cross
ⓑ drive in front of the person
ⓒ drive behind the person
ⓓ sound your horn
ⓔ be patient
ⓕ edge forward slowly

Question 22

As you approach a pelican crossing the lights change to green. Elderly people are halfway across. You should

Mark one answer

ⓐ wave them to cross as quickly as they can
ⓑ rev your engine to make them hurry
ⓒ flash your lights in case they have not heard you
ⓓ wait because they will take longer to cross

Question 23

A toucan crossing is different from other crossings because

Mark one answer

ⓐ moped riders can use it
ⓑ it is controlled by a traffic warden
ⓒ it is controlled by two flashing lights
ⓓ cyclists can use it

Question 24

At toucan crossings

Mark two answers

ⓐ there is no flashing amber light
ⓑ cyclists are not permitted
ⓒ there is a continuously flashing amber beacon
ⓓ pedestrians and cyclists may cross
ⓔ you only stop if someone is waiting to cross

Question 25

You are driving past parked cars. You notice a wheel of a bicycle sticking out between them. What should you do?

Mark one answer

ⓐ Accelerate past quickly and sound your horn
ⓑ Slow down and wave the cyclist across
ⓒ Brake sharply and flash your headlights
ⓓ Slow down and be prepared to stop for a cyclist

Question 26

You are driving past a line of parked cars. You notice a ball bouncing out into the road ahead. What should you do?

Mark one answer

ⓐ Continue driving at the same speed and sound your horn
ⓑ Continue driving at the same speed and flash your headlights
ⓒ Slow down and be prepared to stop for children
ⓓ Stop and wave the children across to fetch their ball

Question 27

What does this sign tell you?

Mark one answer

ⓐ No cycling
ⓑ Cycle route ahead
ⓒ Route for cycles only
ⓓ End of cycle route

Question 28

How will a school-crossing patrol signal you to stop?

Mark one answer

- ⓐ By pointing to children on the opposite pavement
- ⓑ By displaying a red light
- ⓒ By displaying a stop sign
- ⓓ By giving you an arm signal

Question 29

Where would you see this sign?

Mark one answer

- ⓐ In the window of a car taking children to school
- ⓑ At the side of the road
- ⓒ At playground areas
- ⓓ On the rear of a school bus or coach

Question 30

Where would you see this sign?

Mark one answer

- ⓐ Near a school crossing
- ⓑ At a playground entrance
- ⓒ On a school bus
- ⓓ At a 'pedestrians only' area

Question 31

You are parking your vehicle in the street. The car parked in front of you is displaying an orange badge. You should

Mark one answer

- ⓐ park close to it to save road space
- ⓑ allow room for a wheelchair
- ⓒ wait until the orange-badge holder returns
- ⓓ park with two wheels on the pavement

Question 32

You are following a car driven by an elderly driver. You should

Mark one answer

- ⓐ expect the driver to drive badly
- ⓑ flash your lights and overtake
- ⓒ be aware that the driver's reactions may not be as fast as yours
- ⓓ stay very close behind but be careful

Question 33

Which sign tells you that pedestrians may be walking in the road as there is no pavement?

Mark one answer

a

b

c

d

Question 34

What does this sign mean?

Mark one answer

a No route for pedestrians and cyclists

b A route for pedestrians only

c A route for cyclists only

d A route for pedestrians and cyclists

Question 35

You see a pedestrian with a white stick and red band. This means that the person is

Mark one answer

a physically disabled

b deaf only

c blind only

d deaf and blind

Question 36

You are driving towards a zebra crossing. Waiting to cross is a person in a wheelchair. You should

Mark one answer

a continue on your way

b wave to the person to cross

c wave to the person to wait

d be prepared to stop

Question 37

What action would you take when elderly people are crossing the road?

Mark one answer

a Wave them across so they know that you have seen them

b Be patient and allow them to cross in their own time

c Rev the engine to let them know that you are waiting

d Tap the horn in case they are hard of hearing

Question 38

You see two elderly pedestrians about to cross the road ahead. You should

Mark one answer

ⓐ expect them to wait for you to pass

ⓑ speed up to get past them quickly

ⓒ stop and wave them across the road

ⓓ be careful, they may misjudge your speed

Question 39

You are following a motorcyclist on an uneven road. You should

Mark one answer

ⓐ allow less room so you can be seen in their mirrors

ⓑ overtake immediately

ⓒ allow extra room in case they swerve to avoid pot-holes

ⓓ allow the same room as normal because road surfaces do not affect motorcyclists

Question 40

What does this sign mean?

Mark one answer

ⓐ Contra-flow pedal cycle lane

ⓑ With-flow pedal cycle lane

ⓒ Pedal cycles and buses only

ⓓ No pedal cycles or buses

Question 41

You should NEVER attempt to overtake a cyclist

Mark one answer

ⓐ just before you turn left

ⓑ just before you turn right

ⓒ on a one-way street

ⓓ on a dual carriageway

Question 42

You are following a cyclist. You wish to turn left just ahead. You should

Mark one answer

ⓐ overtake the cyclist before the junction

ⓑ pull alongside the cyclist and stay level until after the junction

ⓒ hold back until the cyclist has passed the junction

ⓓ go around the cyclist on the junction

Question 43

You are coming up to a roundabout. A cyclist is signalling to turn right. What should you do?

Mark one answer

- ⓐ Overtake on the right
- ⓑ Give a horn warning
- ⓒ Signal the cyclist to move across
- ⓓ Give the cyclist plenty of room

Question 44

You are following two cyclists. They approach a roundabout in the left-hand lane. In which direction should you expect the cyclists to go?

Mark one answer

- ⓐ Left
- ⓑ Right
- ⓒ Any direction
- ⓓ Straight ahead

Question 45

You are approaching this roundabout and see the cyclist signal right. Why is the cyclist keeping to the left?

Mark one answer

- ⓐ It is a quicker route for the cyclist
- ⓑ The cyclist is going to turn left instead
- ⓒ The cyclist thinks *The Highway Code* does not apply to bicycles
- ⓓ The cyclist is slower and more vulnerable

Question 46

When you are overtaking a cyclist you should leave as much room as you would give to a car. What is the main reason for this?

Mark one answer

- ⓐ The cyclist might change lanes
- ⓑ The cyclist might get off the bike
- ⓒ The cyclist might swerve
- ⓓ The cyclist might have to make a right turn

Question 47

Which TWO should you allow extra room when overtaking?

Mark two answers

ⓐ Motorcycles

ⓑ Tractors

ⓒ Bicycles

ⓓ Road-sweeping vehicles

Question 48

Why should you allow extra room when overtaking a motorcyclist on a windy day?

Mark one answer

ⓐ The rider may turn off suddenly to get out of the wind

ⓑ The rider may be blown across in front of you

ⓒ The rider may stop suddenly

ⓓ The rider may be travelling faster than normal

Question 49

Why should you look particularly for motorcyclists and cyclists at junctions?

Mark one answer

ⓐ They may want to turn into the side road

ⓑ They may slow down to let you turn

ⓒ They are harder to see

ⓓ They might not see you turn

Question 50

You are waiting to come out of a side road. Why should you watch carefully for motorcycles?

Mark one answer

ⓐ Motorcycles are usually faster than cars

ⓑ Police patrols often use motorcycles

ⓒ Motorcycles are small and hard to see

ⓓ Motorcycles have right of way

Question 51

Where should you take particular care to look out for motorcyclists and cyclists?

Mark one answer

ⓐ On dual carriageways

ⓑ At junctions

ⓒ At zebra crossings

ⓓ On one-way streets

Question 52

In daylight, an approaching motorcyclist is using a dipped headlight. Why?

Mark one answer

ⓐ So that the rider can be seen more easily

ⓑ To stop the battery overcharging

ⓒ To improve the rider's vision

ⓓ The rider is inviting you to proceed

Question 53

Where in particular should you look out for motorcyclists?

Mark one answer

ⓐ In a filling station
ⓑ At a road junction
ⓒ Near a service area
ⓓ When entering a car park

Question 54

Motorcyclists should wear bright clothing mainly because

Mark one answer

ⓐ they must do so by law
ⓑ it helps keep them cool in summer
ⓒ the colours are popular
ⓓ drivers often do not see them

Question 55

There is a slow-moving motorcyclist ahead of you. You are unsure what the rider is going to do. You should

Mark one answer

ⓐ pass on the left
ⓑ pass on the right
ⓒ stay behind
ⓓ move closer

Question 56

You are travelling behind a moped. You want to turn left just ahead.
You should

Mark one answer

ⓐ overtake the moped before the junction
ⓑ pull alongside the moped and stay level until just before the junction
ⓒ sound your horn as a warning and pull in front of the moped
ⓓ stay behind until the moped has passed the junction

Question 57

Motorcyclists will often look round over their right shoulder just before turning right. This is because

Mark one answer

ⓐ they need to listen for following traffic
ⓑ motorcycles do not have mirrors
ⓒ looking around helps them balance as they turn
ⓓ they need to check for traffic in their blind area

Question 58

At road junctions which of the following are most vulnerable?

Mark three answers

ⓐ Cyclists
ⓑ Motorcyclists
ⓒ Pedestrians
ⓓ Car drivers
ⓔ Lorry drivers

Question 59

You want to turn right from a main road into a side road. Just before turning you should

Mark one answer

ⓐ cancel your right-turn signal
ⓑ select first gear
ⓒ check for traffic overtaking on your right
ⓓ stop and set the handbrake

Question 60

Motorcyclists are particularly vulnerable

Mark one answer

ⓐ when moving off
ⓑ on dual carriageways
ⓒ when approaching junctions
ⓓ on motorways

Question 61

Which THREE of the following are hazards motorcyclists present in queues of traffic?

Mark three answers

ⓐ Cutting in just in front of you
ⓑ Riding in single file
ⓒ Passing very close to you
ⓓ Riding with their headlight on dipped beam
ⓔ Filtering between the lanes

Question 62

You are driving on a main road. You intend to turn right into a side road. Just before turning you should

Mark one answer

ⓐ adjust your interior mirror
ⓑ flash your headlamps
ⓒ steer over to the left
ⓓ check for traffic overtaking on your right

Question 63

Ahead of you there is a vehicle with a flashing amber beacon. This means it is

Mark one answer

ⓐ slow moving
ⓑ broken down
ⓒ a doctor's car
ⓓ a school-crossing patrol

Question 64

You are driving in slow-moving queues of traffic. Just before changing lane you should

Mark one answer

ⓐ sound the horn
ⓑ look for motorcyclists filtering through the traffic
ⓒ give a 'slowing down' arm signal
ⓓ change down to first gear

Question 65

An injured motorcyclist is lying unconscious in the road. You should

Mark one answer

ⓐ remove the safety helmet
ⓑ seek medical assistance
ⓒ move the person off the road
ⓓ remove the leather jacket

Question 66

You are riding on a country lane. You see cattle on the road. You should

Mark three answers

ⓐ slow down
ⓑ stop if necessary
ⓒ give plenty of room
ⓓ rev your engine
ⓔ sound your horn
ⓕ ride up close behind them

Question 67

You are driving in town. There is a bus at the bus stop on the other side of the road. Why should you be careful?

Mark one answer

ⓐ The bus may have broken down
ⓑ Pedestrians may come from behind the bus
ⓒ The bus may move off suddenly
ⓓ The bus may remain stationary

Question 68

You are about to overtake horse riders. Which TWO of the following could scare the horses?

Mark two answers

ⓐ Sounding your horn
ⓑ Giving arm signals
ⓒ Riding slowly
ⓓ Revving your engine

Question 69

How should you overtake horse riders?

Mark one answer

- ⓐ Drive up close and overtake as soon as possible
- ⓑ Speed is not important but allow plenty of room
- ⓒ Use your horn just once to warn them
- ⓓ Drive slowly and leave plenty of room

Question 70

You notice horse riders in front. What should you do FIRST?

Mark one answer

- ⓐ Pull out to the middle of the road
- ⓑ Be prepared to slow down
- ⓒ Accelerate around them
- ⓓ Signal right

Question 71

You are on a narrow country road. Where would you find it most difficult to see horses and riders ahead of you?

Mark one answer

- ⓐ On left-hand bends
- ⓑ When travelling downhill
- ⓒ When travelling uphill
- ⓓ On right-hand bends

Question 72

A horse rider is in the left-hand lane approaching a roundabout. You should expect the rider to

Mark one answer

- ⓐ go in any direction
- ⓑ turn right
- ⓒ turn left
- ⓓ go ahead

Question 73

You are approaching a roundabout. There are horses just ahead of you. You should

Mark two answers

- ⓐ be prepared to stop
- ⓑ treat them like any other vehicle
- ⓒ give them plenty of room
- ⓓ accelerate past as quickly as possible
- ⓔ sound your horn as a warning

Question 74

You see a horse rider as you approach a roundabout. They are signalling right but keeping well to the left. You should

Mark one answer

ⓐ proceed as normal
ⓑ keep close to them
ⓒ cut in front of them
ⓓ stay well back

Question 75

Which THREE should you do when passing sheep on a road?

Mark three answers

ⓐ Allow plenty of room
ⓑ Go very slowly
ⓒ Pass quickly but quietly
ⓓ Be ready to stop
ⓔ Briefly sound your horn

Question 76

You have a collision whilst your car is moving. What is the first thing you must do?

Mark one answer

ⓐ Stop only if there are injured people
ⓑ Call the emergency services
ⓒ Stop at the scene of the accident
ⓓ Call your insurance company

Question 77

Riders are more likely to have a serious accident if they

Mark one answer

ⓐ wear glasses or contact lenses
ⓑ have recently passed their test
ⓒ are carrying pillion passengers
ⓓ have not taken a theory test

Question 78

How would you react to drivers who appear to be inexperienced?

Mark one answer

ⓐ Sound your horn to warn them of your presence
ⓑ Be patient and prepare for them to react more slowly
ⓒ Flash your headlights to indicate that it is safe for them to proceed
ⓓ Overtake them as soon as possible

Question 79

You have just passed your test. How can you decrease your risk of accidents on the motorway?

Mark one answer

- ⓐ By keeping up with the car in front
- ⓑ By never going over 40 mph
- ⓒ By staying only in the left-hand lane
- ⓓ By taking further training

Question 80

Which age group is most likely to be involved in a road accident?

Mark one answer

- ⓐ 36 to 45-year-olds
- ⓑ 55-year-olds and over
- ⓒ 46 to 55-year-olds
- ⓓ 17 to 25-year-olds

Question 81

You are following a learner driver who stalls at a junction. You should

Mark one answer

- ⓐ be patient as you expect them to make mistakes
- ⓑ stay very close behind and flash your headlights
- ⓒ start to rev your engine if they take too long to restart
- ⓓ immediately steer around them and drive on

Question 82

A learner driver has begun to emerge into your path from a side road on the left. You should

Mark one answer

- ⓐ be ready to slow down and stop
- ⓑ let them emerge then ride close behind
- ⓒ turn into the side road
- ⓓ brake hard, then wave them out

Question 83

The vehicle ahead is being driven by a learner. You should

Mark one answer

- ⓐ keep calm and be patient
- ⓑ ride up close behind
- ⓒ put your headlight on full beam
- ⓓ sound your horn and overtake

Question 84

A friend wants to teach you to drive a car. They must

Mark one answer

- ⓐ be over 21 and have held a full licence for at least two years
- ⓑ be over 18 and hold an advanced driver's certificate
- ⓒ be over 18 and have fully comprehensive insurance
- ⓓ be over 21 and have held a full licence for at least three years

Question 85

At night you see a pedestrian wearing reflective clothing and carrying a bright red light. What does this mean?

Mark one answer

ⓐ You are approaching roadworks

ⓑ You are approaching an organised walk

ⓒ You are approaching a slow-moving vehicle

ⓓ You are approaching an accident black spot

Question 86

You are dazzled at night by a vehicle behind you. You should

Mark one answer

ⓐ set your mirror to anti dazzle

ⓑ set your mirror to dazzle the other driver

ⓒ brake sharply to a stop

ⓓ switch your rear lights on and off

Question 87

There are flashing amber lights under a school warning sign. What action should you take?

Mark one answer

ⓐ Reduce speed until you are clear of the area

ⓑ Keep up your speed and sound the horn

ⓒ Increase your speed to clear the area quickly

ⓓ Wait at the lights until they change to green

Question 88

Why is it vital for a rider to make a lifesaver check before turning right?

Mark one answer

ⓐ To check for any overtaking traffic

ⓑ To confirm that they are about to turn

ⓒ To make sure the side road is clear

ⓓ To check that the rear indicator is flashing

Question 89

Which of the following types of crossing can detect when people are on them?

Mark one answer

- a) Pelican
- b) Toucan
- c) Zebra
- d) Puffin

Question 90

The road outside this school is marked with yellow zigzag lines. What do these lines mean?

Mark one answer

- a) You may park on the lines when dropping off school children
- b) You may park on the lines when picking school children up
- c) You must not wait or park your vehicle here at all
- d) You must stay with your vehicle if you park here

Question 91

You are approaching this crossing. You should

Mark one answer

- a) prepare to slow down and stop
- b) stop and wave the pedestrians across
- c) speed up and pass by quickly
- d) drive on unless the pedestrians step out

Question 92

You see a pedestrian with a dog. The dog has a bright orange lead and collar. This especially warns you that the pedestrian is

Mark one answer

- a) elderly
- b) dog training
- c) colour blind
- d) deaf

Q001 d

Q002 a

Q003 b

Q004 c Pedestrians are the most likely to expect as country roads often have no pavements and pedestrians are advised to walk on the right so that they can see oncoming traffic on their side of the road. However, you should always expect the unexpected when driving.

Q005 d Red triangles give warnings, in this case of people walking along the road. 'c' is a warning of a pedestrian crossing.

Q006 d When you turn into a side road pedestrians who are already crossing have priority so you must give way.

Q007 d

Q008 c

Q009 c

Q010 b

Q011 b

Q012 b

Q013 d Children are small and you may not be able to see them through your rear windscreen.

Q014 c

Q015 d

Q016 c You cannot turn right until you can see it is safe to do so. You should stop and then edge slowly forwards until you can see clearly to the left and right.

Q017 b

Q018 a,b,e

Q019 a,d,e

Q020 c

Q021 a,e

Q022 d

Q023 d

Q024 a,d

Q025 d

Q026 c

Q027 b

Q028 c

Q029 d

Q030 c

Q031 b

Q032 c

Q033 a

Q034 d

Q035 d

Q036 d

Q037 b

Q038 d The ability to judge speed tends to deteriorate as you get older.

Q039 c

Q040 b

Q041 a The word 'NEVER' makes 'a' correct.

Q042 c As the question states you are turning left JUST ahead, you have no time to overtake the cyclist safely which is why 'c' is correct.

Q043 d

Q044 c

Q045 d

Answers and explanations

Q046 c 'c' is the answer required, but you should also be aware that cyclists can be unpredictable.

Q047 a,c

Motorcycles and bicycles can easily swerve and you need to allow them extra room.

Q048 b

Q049 c

Q050 c

Q051 b

Q052 a

Q053 b

Q054 d

Q055 c

Q056 d

Q057 d

Q058 a,b,c

Q059 c Use your right door mirror and look particularly for motorcyclists.

Q060 c

Q061 a,c,e

Check your door mirrors, especially before moving forwards or changing lanes.

Q062 d

Q063 a

Q064 b

Q065 b

Q066 a,b,c

Q067 b

Q068 a,d

Q069 d

Q070 b Horses and their riders can be unpredictable so 'b' is the safest first action.

Q071 a

Q072 a 'a' is correct. However, remember that narrow country roads often have banks, hedges, trees or other obstructions to your view as well as bends so look out on right-hand bends as well.

Q073 a,c

Q074 d

Q075 a,b,d

Q076 c

Q077 b

Q078 b

Q079 d

Q080 d

Q081 a

Q082 a

Q083 a

Q084 d

Q085 b

Q086 a

Q087 a

Q088 a

Q089 d

Q090 c

Q091 a

Q092 d

Driving Theory
Test
Questions
2000/2001

Other Types of Vehicle

We won't fail you

Question 1

The road is wet. Why might a motorcyclist steer round drain covers on a bend?

Mark one answer

ⓐ To avoid puncturing the tyres on the edge of the drain covers

ⓑ To prevent the motorcycle sliding on the metal drain covers

ⓒ To help judge the bend using the drain covers as marker points

ⓓ To avoid splashing pedestrians on the pavement

Question 2

It is very windy. You are behind a motorcyclist who is overtaking a high-sided vehicle. What should you do?

Mark one answer

ⓐ Overtake the motorcyclist immediately

ⓑ Keep well back

ⓒ Stay level with the motorcyclist

ⓓ Keep close to the motorcyclist

Question 3

It is very windy. You are about to overtake a motorcyclist. You should

Mark one answer

ⓐ overtake slowly

ⓑ allow extra room

ⓒ sound your horn

ⓓ keep close as you pass

Question 4

You are about to overtake a slow-moving motorcyclist. Which one of these signs would make you take special care?

Mark one answer

ⓐ   ⓑ

ⓒ   ⓓ

Question 5

You are waiting to emerge left from a minor road. A large vehicle is approaching from the right. You have time to turn, but you should wait. Why?

Mark one answer

ⓐ The large vehicle can easily hide an overtaking vehicle

ⓑ The large vehicle can turn suddenly

ⓒ The large vehicle is difficult to steer in a straight line

ⓓ The large vehicle can easily hide vehicles from the left

Question 6

You are following a large articulated vehicle. It is going to turn left into a narrow road. What action should you take?

Mark one answer

- ⓐ Move out and overtake on the right
- ⓑ Pass on the left as the vehicle moves out
- ⓒ Be prepared to stop behind
- ⓓ Overtake quickly before the lorry moves out

Question 7

You are following a long vehicle. It approaches a crossroads and signals left, but moves out to the right. You should

Mark one answer

- ⓐ get closer in order to pass it quickly
- ⓑ stay well back and give it room
- ⓒ assume the signal is wrong and it is really turning right
- ⓓ overtake as it starts to slow down

Question 8

You are riding behind a long vehicle. There is a mini-roundabout ahead. The vehicle is signalling left, but positioned to the right. You should

Mark one answer

- ⓐ sound your horn
- ⓑ overtake on the left
- ⓒ keep well back
- ⓓ flash your headlights

Question 9

You are following a long vehicle approaching a crossroads. The driver signals right but moves close to the left-hand kerb. What should you do?

Mark one answer

- ⓐ Warn the driver of the wrong signal
- ⓑ Wait behind the long vehicle
- ⓒ Report the driver to the police
- ⓓ Overtake on the right-hand side

Question 10

You are approaching a mini-roundabout. The long vehicle in front is signalling left but positioned over to the right.
You should

Mark one answer

- a sound your horn
- b overtake on the left
- c follow the same course as the lorry
- d keep well back

Question 11

You are following a large vehicle. Side and end markers are being displayed. This means the load

Mark one answer

- a is higher than normal
- b may be flammable
- c is in two parts
- d overhangs at the rear

Question 12

You are towing a caravan. Which is the safest type of rear-view mirror to use?

Mark one answer

- a Interior wide-angle-view mirror
- b Extended-arm side mirrors
- c Ordinary door mirrors
- d Ordinary interior mirror

Question 13

You keep well back while waiting to overtake a large vehicle. A car fills the gap. You should

Mark one answer

- a sound your horn
- b drop back further
- c flash your headlights
- d start to overtake

Question 14

Before overtaking a large vehicle you should keep well back. Why is this?

Mark one answer

- a To give acceleration space to overtake quickly on blind bends
- b To get the best view of the road ahead
- c To leave a gap in case the vehicle stops and rolls back
- d To offer other drivers a safe gap if they want to overtake you

Question 15

You wish to overtake a long, slow-moving vehicle on a busy road. You should

Mark one answer

[a] follow it closely and keep moving out to see the road ahead

[b] flash your headlights for the oncoming traffic to give way

[c] stay behind until the driver waves you past

[d] keep well back until you can see that it is clear

Question 16

You are driving downhill. There is a car parked on the other side of the road. Large, slow lorries are coming towards you. You should

Mark one answer

[a] keep going because you have the right of way

[b] slow down and give way

[c] speed up and get past quickly

[d] pull over on the right behind the parked car

Question 17

Why is passing a lorry more risky than passing a car?

Mark one answer

[a] Lorries are longer than cars

[b] Lorries may suddenly pull up

[c] The brakes of lorries are not as good

[d] Lorries climb hills more slowly

Question 18

As a driver, why should you be more careful where trams operate?

Mark two answers

[a] Because they do not have a horn

[b] Because they do not stop for cars

[c] Because they are silent

[d] Because they cannot steer to avoid you

[e] Because they do not have lights

Question 19

You are driving along a road and you see this signal. It means

Mark one answer

[a] cars must stop

[b] trams must stop

[c] both trams and cars must stop

[d] both trams and cars can continue

Question 20

You are travelling behind a bus that pulls up at a bus stop. What should you do?

Mark two answers

[a] Accelerate past the bus sounding your horn

[b] Watch carefully for pedestrians

[c] Be ready to give way to the bus

[d] Pull in closely behind the bus

Question 21

You are driving in town. Ahead of you a bus is at a bus stop. Which TWO of the following should you do?

Mark two answers

- ⓐ Be prepared to give way if the bus suddenly moves off
- ⓑ Continue at the same speed but sound your horn as a warning
- ⓒ Watch carefully for the sudden appearance of pedestrians
- ⓓ Pass the bus as quickly as you possibly can

Question 22

When you approach a bus signalling to move off from a bus stop you should

Mark one answer

- ⓐ get past before it moves
- ⓑ allow it to pull away, if it is safe to do so
- ⓒ flash your headlights as you approach
- ⓓ signal left and wave the bus on

Question 23

Which of these vehicles is LEAST likely to be affected by crosswinds?

Mark one answer

- ⓐ Cyclists
- ⓑ Motorcyclists
- ⓒ High-sided vehicles
- ⓓ Cars

Question 24

You are following a large lorry on a wet road. Spray makes it difficult to see. You should

Mark one answer

- ⓐ drop back until you can see better
- ⓑ put your headlights on full beam
- ⓒ keep close to the lorry, away from the spray
- ⓓ speed up and overtake quickly

Question 25

You are on a wet motorway with surface spray. You should use

Mark one answer

- ⓐ hazard flashers
- ⓑ dipped headlights
- ⓒ rear fog lights
- ⓓ sidelights

Question 26

You are driving in heavy traffic on a wet road. Spray makes it difficult to be seen. You should use your

Mark two answers

ⓐ full beam headlights

ⓑ rear fog lights if visibility is less than 100 metres (328 feet)

ⓒ rear fog lights if visibility is more than 100 metres (328 feet)

ⓓ dipped headlights

ⓔ sidelights only

Question 27

Some two-way roads are divided into three lanes. Why are these particularly dangerous?

Mark one answer

ⓐ Traffic in both directions can use the middle lane to overtake

ⓑ Traffic can travel faster in poor weather conditions

ⓒ Traffic can overtake on the left

ⓓ Traffic uses the middle lane for emergencies only

Question 28

Why should you be careful when riding on roads where electric trams operate?

Mark two answers

ⓐ They cannot steer to avoid you

ⓑ They move quickly and quietly

ⓒ They are noisy and slow

ⓓ They can steer to avoid you

ⓔ They give off harmful exhaust fumes

Question 29

You are driving along this road. What should you be prepared to do?

Mark one answer

ⓐ Sound your horn and continue

ⓑ Slow down and give way

ⓒ Report the driver to the police

ⓓ Squeeze through the gap

Question 30

What should you do as you approach this lorry?

Mark one answer

- a Slow down and be prepared to wait
- b Make the lorry wait for you
- c Flash your lights at the lorry
- d Move to the right-hand side of the road

Answers and explanations

Q001   b Water on metal is a dangerous combination, especially for a two-wheeled vehicle.

Q002   b Let the motorcyclist complete the overtake before even thinking about following.

Q003   b Motorcycles may have problems with strong crosswinds.

Q004   a The motorcyclist may wobble as you pass by in a windy situation.

Q005   a

Q006   c The large articulated vehicle may need to position to the right in order to turn left into the narrow road.

Q007   b

Q008   c

Q009   b Long vehicles require more space to turn and often need to position for this.

Q010   d

Q011   d

Q012   b

Q013   b

Q014   b

Q015   d

Q016   b

Q017   a Overtaking takes time, so the longer the vehicle you overtake the greater the danger, as you will take longer to pass it.

Q018   c,d

Q019   b

Q020   b,c

Q021   a,c

Q022   b This helps traffic flow without giving confusing signals.

Q023   d Of the four mentioned, cars
        are by far the most stable
        and least affected by
        crosswinds.
Q024   a
Q025   b
Q026   b,d
Q027   a
Q028   a,b
Q029   b
Q030   a

Driving Theory
Test
Questions
2000/2001

Vehicle Handling

BSM
We won't fail you

Question 1

To gain basic skills in how to ride a motorcycle you should

Mark one answer

ⓐ practise off-road with an approved training body

ⓑ ride on the road on the first dry day

ⓒ practise off-road in a public park or in a quiet cul-de-sac

ⓓ ride on the road as soon as possible

Question 2

When you are seated on a stationary motorcycle, your position should allow you to

Mark one answer

ⓐ just touch the ground with your toes

ⓑ place both feet on the ground

ⓒ operate the centre stand

ⓓ reach the switches by stretching

Question 3

As a safety measure before starting your engine, you should

Mark two answers

ⓐ push the motorcycle forward to check the rear wheel turns freely

ⓑ engage first gear and apply the rear brake

ⓒ engage first gear and apply the front brake

ⓓ glance at the neutral light on your instrument panel

Question 4

You should not ride with your clutch lever pulled in for longer than necessary because it

Mark one answer

ⓐ increases wear on the gearbox

ⓑ increases petrol consumption

ⓒ reduces your control of the motorcycle

ⓓ reduces the grip of the tyres

Question 5

What are TWO main reasons why coasting downhill is wrong?

Mark two answers

ⓐ Fuel consumption will be higher

ⓑ The vehicle will pick up speed

ⓒ It puts more wear and tear on the tyres

ⓓ You have less braking and steering control

ⓔ It damages the engine

Question 6

Why is coasting wrong?

Mark one answer

ⓐ It will cause the car to skid

ⓑ It will make the engine stall

ⓒ The engine will run faster

ⓓ There is no engine braking

Question 7

Hills can affect the performance of your vehicle. Which TWO apply when driving up steep hills?

Mark two answers

ⓐ Higher gears will pull better

ⓑ You will slow down sooner

ⓒ Overtaking will be easier

ⓓ The engine will work harder

ⓔ The steering will feel heavier

Question 8

You should brake

Mark one answer

ⓐ by using the rear brake first and then the front

ⓑ when the machine is being turned or ridden through a bend

ⓒ by pulling in the clutch before using the front brake

ⓓ when the machine is upright and moving in a straight line

Question 9

You are following a vehicle at a safe distance on a wet road. Another driver overtakes you and pulls into the gap you have left. What should you do?

Mark one answer

ⓐ Flash your headlights as a warning

ⓑ Try to overtake safely as soon as you can

ⓒ Drop back to regain a safe distance

ⓓ Stay close to the other vehicle until it moves on

Question 10

In which THREE of these situations may you overtake another vehicle on the left?

Mark three answers

ⓐ When you are in a one-way street

ⓑ When approaching a motorway slip road where you will be turning off

ⓒ When the vehicle in front is signalling to turn right

ⓓ When a slower vehicle is travelling in the right-hand lane of a dual carriageway

ⓔ In slow-moving traffic queues when traffic in the right-hand lane is moving more slowly

Question 11

You are driving on the motorway in windy conditions. When passing high-sided vehicles you should

Mark one answer

- (a) increase your speed
- (b) be wary of a sudden gust
- (c) drive alongside very closely
- (d) expect normal conditions

Question 12

When coming to a normal stop on a motorcycle, you should

Mark one answer

- (a) only apply the front brake
- (b) rely just on the rear brake
- (c) apply both brakes smoothly
- (d) apply either of the brakes gently

Question 13

Which THREE of the following will affect your stopping distance?

Mark three answers

- (a) How fast you are going
- (b) The tyres on your vehicle
- (c) The time of day
- (d) The weather
- (e) The street lighting

Question 14

You are travelling in very heavy rain. Your overall stopping distance is likely to be

Mark one answer

- (a) doubled
- (b) halved
- (c) up to ten times greater
- (d) no different

Question 15

You are approaching this junction. As the motorcyclist you should

Mark two answers

- (a) prepare to slow down
- (b) sound your horn
- (c) keep near the left kerb
- (d) speed up to clear the junction
- (e) stop, as the car has right of way

Question 16

What can you do to improve your safety on the road as a motorcyclist?

Mark one answer

[a] Anticipate the actions of others

[b] Stay just above the speed limits

[c] Keep positioned close to the kerbs

[d] Remain well below speed limits

Question 17

Which FOUR types of road surface increase the risk of skidding for motorcyclists?

Mark four answers

[a] White lines

[b] Dry tarmac

[c] Tar banding

[d] Yellow grid lines

[e] Loose chippings

Question 18

You have to brake sharply and your machine starts to skid. You should

Mark one answer

[a] continue braking and select a low gear

[b] apply the brakes harder for better grip

[c] select neutral and use the front brake only

[d] release the brakes and re-apply

Question 19

Which THREE of these can cause skidding?

Mark three answers

[a] Braking too gently

[b] Leaning too far over when cornering

[c] Staying upright when cornering

[d] Braking too hard

[e] Changing direction suddenly

Question 20

To correct a rear-wheel skid you should

Mark one answer

[a] not steer at all

[b] steer away from it

[c] steer into it

[d] apply your handbrake

Question 21

It is very cold and the road looks wet. You cannot hear any road noise. You should

Mark two answers

[a] continue riding at the same speed

[b] ride slower in as high a gear as possible

[c] ride in as low a gear as possible

[d] keep revving your engine

[e] slow down as there may be black ice

Question 22

You are approaching a road with a surface of loose chippings. What should you do?

Mark one answer

ⓐ Ride normally
ⓑ Speed up
ⓒ Slow down
ⓓ Stop suddenly

Question 23

When snow is falling heavily you should

Mark one answer

ⓐ drive as long as your headlights are used
ⓑ not drive unless you have a mobile phone
ⓒ drive only when your journey is short
ⓓ not drive unless it is essential

Question 24

You are driving on an icy road. What distance should you drive from the car in front?

Mark one answer

ⓐ four times the normal distance
ⓑ six times the normal distance
ⓒ eight times the normal distance
ⓓ ten times the normal distance

Question 25

You are driving in very wet weather. Your vehicle begins to slide. This effect is called

Mark one answer

ⓐ hosing
ⓑ weaving
ⓒ aquaplaning
ⓓ fading

Question 26

Why should you test your brakes after this hazard?

Mark one answer

ⓐ Because you will be on a slippery road
ⓑ Because your brakes will be soaking wet
ⓒ Because you will have gone down a long hill
ⓓ Because you will have just crossed a long bridge

Question 27

You have to make a journey in fog. What are the TWO most important things you should do before you set out?

Mark two answers

- ⓐ Top up the radiator with antifreeze
- ⓑ Make sure that you have a warning triangle in the vehicle
- ⓒ Check that your lights are working
- ⓓ Check the battery
- ⓔ Make sure that the windows are clean

Question 28

When riding a motorcycle you should wear full protective clothing

Mark one answer

- ⓐ at all times
- ⓑ only on faster, open roads
- ⓒ just on long journeys
- ⓓ only during bad weather

Question 29

You have to make a journey in fog. What are the TWO most important things you should do before you set out?

Mark two answers

- ⓐ Fill up with fuel
- ⓑ Make sure that you have a warm drink with you
- ⓒ Check that your lights are working
- ⓓ Check the battery
- ⓔ Make sure that your visor is clean

Question 30

You have to make a journey in foggy conditions. You should

Mark one answer

- ⓐ follow closely other vehicles' tail lights
- ⓑ avoid using dipped headlights
- ⓒ leave plenty of time for your journey
- ⓓ keep two seconds behind other vehicles

Question 31

Front fog lights may be used ONLY if

Mark one answer

- ⓐ visibility is seriously reduced
- ⓑ they are fitted above the bumper
- ⓒ they are not as bright as the headlights
- ⓓ an audible warning device is used

Question 32

Front fog lights may be used ONLY if

Mark one answer

- ⓐ your headlights are not working
- ⓑ they are operated with rear fog lights
- ⓒ they were fitted by the vehicle manufacturer
- ⓓ visibility is seriously reduced

Question 33

You may drive with front fog lights switched-on

Mark one answer

a) when visibility is less than 100 metres (328 feet)
b) at any time to be noticed
c) instead of headlights on high speed roads
d) when dazzled by the lights of oncoming vehicles

Question 34

Front fog lights should be used ONLY when

Mark one answer

a) travelling in very light rain
b) visibility is seriously reduced
c) daylight is fading
d) driving after midnight

Question 35

Front fog lights should be used

Mark one answer

a) when visibility is reduced to 100 metres (328 feet)
b) as a warning to oncoming traffic
c) when driving during the hours of darkness
d) in any conditions and at any time

Question 36

Using front fog lights in clear daylight will

Mark one answer

a) flatten the battery
b) dazzle other drivers
c) improve your visibility
d) increase your awareness

Question 37

You may use front fog lights with headlights ONLY when visibility is reduced to less than

Mark one answer

a) 100 metres (328 feet)
b) 200 metres (656 feet)
c) 300 metres (984 feet)
d) 400 metres (1312 feet)

Question 38

You are following other vehicles in fog with your lights on. How else can you reduce the chances of being involved in an accident?

Mark one answer

ⓐ Keep close to the vehicle in front
ⓑ Use your main beam instead of dipped headlights
ⓒ Keep together with the faster vehicles
ⓓ Reduce your speed and increase the gap

Question 39

Why should you always reduce your speed when travelling in fog?

Mark one answer

ⓐ Because the brakes do not work as well
ⓑ Because you could be dazzled by other people's fog lights
ⓒ Because the engine is colder
ⓓ Because it is more difficult to see events ahead

Question 40

You are driving in fog. Why should you keep well back from the vehicle in front?

Mark one answer

ⓐ In case it changes direction suddenly
ⓑ In case its fog lights dazzle you
ⓒ In case it stops suddenly
ⓓ In case its brake lights dazzle you

Question 41

You should switch your rear fog lights on when visibility drops below

Mark one answer

ⓐ your overall stopping distance
ⓑ ten car lengths
ⓒ 200 metres (656 feet)
ⓓ 100 metres (328 feet)

Question 42

Using rear fog lights in clear daylight will

Mark one answer

ⓐ be useful when towing a trailer
ⓑ give extra protection
ⓒ dazzle other drivers
ⓓ make following drivers keep back

Question 43

You are driving on a clear, dry night with your rear fog lights switched on.
This may

Mark two answers

ⓐ reduce glare from the road surface
ⓑ make other drivers think you are braking
ⓒ give a better view of the road ahead
ⓓ dazzle following drivers
ⓔ help your indicators to be seen more clearly

Question 44

Why is it dangerous to leave rear fog lights on when they are not needed?

Mark two answers

ⓐ Brake lights are less clear

ⓑ Following drivers can be dazzled

ⓒ Electrical systems could be overloaded

ⓓ Direction indicators may not work properly

ⓔ The battery could fail

Question 45

Whilst driving, the fog clears and you can see more clearly. You must remember to

Mark one answer

ⓐ switch off the fog lights

ⓑ reduce your speed

ⓒ switch off the demister

ⓓ close any open windows

Question 46

You have just driven out of fog. Visibility is now good. You MUST

Mark one answer

ⓐ switch off all your fog lights

ⓑ keep your rear fog lights on

ⓒ keep your front fog lights on

ⓓ leave fog lights on in case fog returns

Question 47

You forget to switch off your rear fog lights when the fog has cleared. This may

Mark three answers

ⓐ dazzle other road users

ⓑ reduce battery life

ⓒ cause brake lights to be less clear

ⓓ be breaking the law

ⓔ seriously affect engine power

Question 48

You have been driving in thick fog which has now cleared. You must switch OFF your rear fog lights because

Mark one answer

ⓐ they use a lot of power from the battery

ⓑ they make your brake lights less clear

ⓒ they will cause dazzle in your rear view mirrors

ⓓ they may not be properly adjusted

Question 49

You are driving with your front fog lights switched on. Earlier fog has now cleared. What should you do?

Mark one answer

[a] Leave them on if other drivers have their lights on

[b] Switch them off as long as visibility remains good

[c] Flash them to warn oncoming traffic that it is foggy

[d] Drive with them on instead of your headlights

Question 50

While you are driving in fog, it becomes necessary to use front fog lights.You should

Mark one answer

[a] only turn them on in heavy traffic conditions

[b] remember not to use them on motorways

[c] only use them with dipped headlights

[d] remember to switch them off as visibility improves

Question 51

You have to park on the road in fog. You should

Mark one answer

[a] leave sidelights on

[b] leave dipped headlights and fog lights on

[c] leave dipped headlights on

[d] leave main beam headlights on

Question 52

On a foggy day you unavoidably have to park your car on the road. You should

Mark one answer

[a] leave your headlights on

[b] leave your fog lights on

[c] leave your sidelights on

[d] leave your hazard lights on

Question 53

The best place to park your motorcycle is

Mark one answer

[a] on soft tarmac

[b] on bumpy ground

[c] on grass

[d] on firm, level ground

Question 54

You are on a motorway in fog. The left-hand edge of the motorway can be identified by reflective studs. What colour are they?

Mark one answer

- a Green
- b Amber
- c Red
- d White

Question 55

When riding in windy conditions, you should

Mark one answer

- a stay close to large vehicles
- b keep your speed up
- c keep your speed down
- d stay close to the gutter

Question 56

In normal riding your position on the road should be

Mark one answer

- a about a foot from the kerb
- b about central in your lane
- c on the right of your lane
- d near the centre of the road

Question 57

You are on a well-lit motorway at night. You must

Mark one answer

- a use only your sidelights
- b always use your headlights
- c always use rear fog lights
- d use headlights only in bad weather

Question 58

You are on a motorway at night. You MUST have your headlights switched on unless

Mark one answer

- a there are vehicles close in front of you
- b you are travelling below 50 mph
- c the motorway is lit
- d your vehicle is broken down on the hard shoulder

Question 59

You are on a motorway at night with other vehicles just ahead of you. Which lights should you have on?

Mark one answer

- a Front fog lights
- b Main beam headlights
- c Sidelights only
- d Dipped headlights

Question 60

Which TWO of the following are correct?
When overtaking at night you should

Mark two answers

ⓐ WAIT until a bend so that you can
see the oncoming headlights

ⓑ sound your horn twice before
moving out

ⓒ be careful because you can
see less

ⓓ beware of bends in the road ahead

ⓔ put headlights on full beam

Question 61

You are overtaking a car at night. You
must be sure that

Mark one answer

ⓐ you flash your headlights before
overtaking

ⓑ you select a higher gear

ⓒ you have switched your lights to full
beam before overtaking

ⓓ you do not dazzle other road users

Question 62

When riding at night you should

Mark two answers

ⓐ wear fluorescent clothing

ⓑ ride closer to the vehicle in front

ⓒ keep your goggles or visor clean

ⓓ ride just left of centre

ⓔ use your headlights

Question 63

You are travelling at night. You are
dazzled by headlights coming towards
you. You should

Mark one answer

ⓐ pull down your sun visor

ⓑ slow down or stop

ⓒ switch on your main beam headlights

ⓓ put your hand over your eyes

Question 64

You are parking on a two-way road at
night. The speed limit is 40 mph. You
should park on the

Mark one answer

ⓐ left with sidelights on

ⓑ left with no lights on

ⓒ right with sidelights on

ⓓ right with dipped headlights on

Question 65

You are on a narrow road at night. A
slower-moving vehicle ahead has been
signalling right for some time. What
should you do?

Mark one answer

ⓐ Overtake on the left

ⓑ Flash your headlights before
overtaking

ⓒ Signal right and sound your horn

ⓓ Wait for the signal to be cancelled
before overtaking

Question 66

A rumble device is designed to

Mark two answers

a) give directions

b) prevent cattle escaping

c) alert you to low tyre pressure

d) alert you to a hazard

e) encourage you to reduce speed

Question 67

Which TWO are correct? The passing places on a single-track road are

Mark two answers

a) for taking a rest and break

b) to pull into if an oncoming vehicle wants to proceed

c) for stopping and checking your route

d) to turn around in, if you are lost

e) to pull into if the car behind wants to overtake

Question 68

You see a vehicle coming towards you on a single-track road. You should

Mark one answer

a) go back to the main road

b) do an emergency stop

c) stop at a passing place

d) put on your hazard warning lights

Question 69

Your motorcycle is parked on a two-way road. You should get on from the

Mark one answer

a) right and apply the rear brake

b) left and leave the brakes alone

c) left and apply the front brake

d) right and leave the brakes alone

Question 70

When may you wait in a box junction?

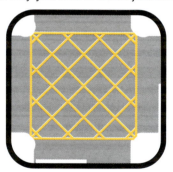

Mark one answer

a) When you are stationary in a queue of traffic

b) When approaching a pelican crossing

c) When approaching a zebra crossing

d) When oncoming traffic prevents you turning right

Question 71

Which of the following may apply when dealing with this hazard?

Mark four answers

- ⓐ It could be more difficult in winter
- ⓑ Use a low gear and drive slowly
- ⓒ Use a high gear to prevent wheelspin
- ⓓ Test your brakes afterwards
- ⓔ Always switch on fog lamps
- ⓕ There may be a depth gauge

Question 72

Which of these plates normally appear with this road sign?

Mark one answer

- ⓐ   Humps for ½ mile
- ⓑ   Hump Bridge
- ⓒ   Low Bridge
- ⓓ   Soft Verge

Question 73

How should a scooter be left when parking for some time in a town centre?

Mark three answers

- ⓐ On firm and level ground
- ⓑ By using the side stand leaning over the kerb
- ⓒ On the centre stand if fitted
- ⓓ Secure and with the fuel tap off
- ⓔ On any very wide pavement

Question 74

You are driving along a road which has speed humps. A driver in front is travelling slower than you. You should

Mark one answer

- ⓐ sound your horn
- ⓑ overtake as soon as you can
- ⓒ flash your headlights
- ⓓ slow down and stay behind

Question 75

Why should motorcyclists ride carefully where trams operate?

Mark two answers

- ⓐ They do not give way to other traffic
- ⓑ They do not have mirrors and will not see you
- ⓒ They do not have lights and might be difficult to see
- ⓓ The rails could affect your steering and braking

Question 76

Areas reserved for trams may have

Mark three answers

- a metal studs around them
- b white line markings
- c zig zag markings
- d a different coloured surface
- e yellow hatch markings
- f a different surface texture

Question 77

It rains after a long dry, hot spell. This may cause the road surface to

Mark one answer

- a be unusually slippery
- b give better grip
- c become covered in grit
- d melt and break up

Question 78

The main causes of a motorcycle skidding are

Mark three answers

- a heavy and sharp braking
- b excessive acceleration
- c leaning too far when cornering
- d riding in wet weather
- e riding in the winter

Question 79

To stop your motorcycle quickly in an emergency you should apply

Mark one answer

- a the rear brake only
- b the front brake only
- c the front brake just before the rear
- d the rear brake just before the front

Question 80

Chains can be fitted to your wheels to help prevent

Mark one answer

- a damage to the road surface
- b wear to the tyres
- c skidding in deep snow
- d the brakes locking

Question 81

Traffic calming measures are used to

Mark one answer

- a stop road rage
- b help overtaking
- c slow traffic down
- d help parking

Answers and explanations

Q001 a

Q002 b

Q003 a,d

Q004 c

Q005 b,d

Q006 d You are coasting when you push down the clutch, disconnecting both engine and gear box.

Q007 b,d

Q008 d Braking at any other time greatly increases the risk of skidding.

Q009 c This may feel irritating, particularly if the circumstance is repeated several times. However, it is safest and, in reality, causes no delay.

Q010 a,c,e

Q011 b

Q012 c In good conditions you should apply greater pressure to the front brake.

Q013 a,b,d

Q014 a

Q015 a,b

Q016 a

Q017 a,c,d,e

Q018 d Your braking is causing the skid, so you must remove the cause by releasing the brakes and then reapplying them.

Q019 b,d,e

Q020 c

Q021 b,e

Q022 c

Q023 d

Q024 d Stopping distances can be up to ten times longer in snow and ice. Give yourself plenty of time to stop.

Q025 c Surface water builds up a film between the road and the tyres, causing the car to drive on the film of water and not grip the road surface. The steering will feel very light if you are aquaplaning.

Q026 b After driving through water your brakes will be wet, and wet brakes are inefficient.

Q027 c,e See and be seen are the two most crucial safety aspects of driving in fog.

Q028 a

Q029 c,e
See and be seen in fog.

Q030 c *The Highway Code* advises you to allow more time for your journey in foggy conditions. However, always ask yourself if the journey really is necessary.

Q031 a

Q032 d

Q033 a

Q034 b

Q035 a

Q036 b

Q037 a

Q038 d

Q039 d Everybody knows this but an alarming number of people don't put the knowledge into practice. Accidents happen as a result.

Q040 c If the car in front stops suddenly you may run into it if you have been driving too close.

Q041 d Remember to switch them off when visibility improves.

Q042 c Always remember to switch off your fog lights as soon as visibility improves.

Q043 b,d

Q044 a,b

Q045 a Fog lights should only be used where visibility is down to about 100 metres. Otherwise you risk dazzling other drivers.

Q046 a

Q047 a,c,d

Q048 b

Q049 b

Q050 d

Q051 a

Q052 c

Q053 d

Q054 c Red reflective studs separate the left-hand lane and the hard shoulder.

Q055 c

Q056 b Your exact position will depend on the width of the road, the road surface, your view ahead and any obstructions.

Q057 b

Q058 d You must use your headlights on motorways at nights even if the motorway is lit.

Answers and explanations

Q059 d Full-beam headlights would dazzle the drivers in front by reflecting in their mirrors.

Q060 c,d

Q061 d You may need to switch to full-beam headlights as you overtake, but not before.

Q062 c,e

Q063 b

Q064 a

Q065 d

Q066 d,e (NB: a rumble device is normally raised strips or markings on the surface of the road.)

Q067 b,e

Q068 c Bear in mind that single-track roads may have passing places at long intervals. You may meet an oncoming vehicle at a point where one of you will need to reverse to the previous nearest passing point.

Q069 c Always mount on the side away from the traffic and apply the front brake to stop the motorcycle moving.

Q070 d You may wait in a box junction if your exit is clear but oncoming traffic prevents you from turning right.

Q071 a,b,d,f

Q072 a

Q073 a,c,d

Q074 d

Q075 a,d

Q076 b,d,f

Q077 a

Q078 a,b,c
       The most common cause of skidding is the actions of the rider.

Q079 c

Q080 c

Q081 c

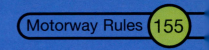

Driving Theory
Test
Questions

2000/2001

Motorway Rules

BSM
We won't fail you

Question 1

As a provisional licence-holder you should not drive a car

Mark one answer

- ⓐ over 50 mph
- ⓑ at night
- ⓒ on the motorway
- ⓓ with passengers in rear seats

Question 2

Which FOUR of these must NOT use motorways?

Mark four answers

- ⓐ Learner car drivers
- ⓑ Motorcycles over 50cc
- ⓒ Double-decker buses
- ⓓ Farm tractors
- ⓔ Horse riders
- ⓕ Cyclists

Question 3

Which FOUR of these must NOT use motorways?

Mark four answers

- ⓐ Learner car drivers
- ⓑ Motorcycles over 50cc
- ⓒ Double-decker buses
- ⓓ Farm tractors
- ⓔ Learner motorcyclists
- ⓕ Cyclists

Question 4

A motorcycle is not allowed on a motorway if it has an engine size smaller than

Mark one answer

- ⓐ 50cc
- ⓑ 125cc
- ⓒ 150cc
- ⓓ 250cc

Question 5

To ride on a motorway your motorcycle must be

Mark one answer

- ⓐ 50cc or more
- ⓑ 100cc or more
- ⓒ 125cc or more
- ⓓ 250cc or more

Question 6

Why is it particularly important to carry out a check on your vehicle before making a long motorway journey?

Mark one answer

- ⓐ You will have to do more harsh braking on motorways
- ⓑ Motorway service stations do not deal with breakdowns
- ⓒ The road surface will wear down the tyres faster
- ⓓ Continuous high speeds may increase the risk of your vehicle breaking down

Question 7

Immediately after joining a motorway you should normally

Mark one answer

ⓐ try to overtake

ⓑ readjust your mirrors

ⓒ position your vehicle in the centre lane

ⓓ keep in the left lane

Question 8

You are joining a motorway. Why is it important to make full use of the slip road?

Mark one answer

ⓐ Because there is space available to turn round if you need to

ⓑ To allow you direct access to the overtaking lanes

ⓒ To build up a speed similar to traffic on the motorway

ⓓ Because you can continue on the hard shoulder

Question 9

You are joining a motorway from a slip road on the left. You should

Mark one answer

ⓐ adjust your speed to the speed of the traffic on the motorway

ⓑ accelerate as quickly as you can and ride straight out

ⓒ ride onto the hard shoulder until a gap appears

ⓓ expect drivers on the motorway to give way to you

Question 10

When joining a motorway you must always

Mark one answer

ⓐ use the hard shoulder

ⓑ stop at the end of the acceleration lane

ⓒ come to a stop before joining the motorway

ⓓ give way to traffic already on the motorway

Question 11

You are riding on a motorway. Unless signs show otherwise you must NOT exceed

Mark one answer

ⓐ 50 mph

ⓑ 60 mph

ⓒ 70 mph

ⓓ 80 mph

Question 12

What is the national speed limit for cars and motorcycles in the centre lane of a three-lane motorway?

Mark one answer

ⓐ 40 mph

ⓑ 50 mph

ⓒ 60 mph

ⓓ 70 mph

Question 13

What is the national speed limit on motorways for cars and motorcycles?

Mark one answer

- ⓐ 30 mph
- ⓑ 50 mph
- ⓒ 60 mph
- ⓓ 70 mph

Question 14

You are towing a trailer on a motorway. What is your maximum speed limit?

Mark one answer

- ⓐ 40 mph
- ⓑ 50 mph
- ⓒ 60 mph
- ⓓ 70 mph

Question 15

You are driving a car on a motorway. Unless signs show otherwise you must NOT exceed

Mark one answer

- ⓐ 50 mph
- ⓑ 60 mph
- ⓒ 70 mph
- ⓓ 80 mph

Question 16

On a three-lane motorway which lane should you normally use?

Mark one answer

- ⓐ Left
- ⓑ Right
- ⓒ Centre
- ⓓ Either the right or centre

Question 17

A basic rule when on motorways is

Mark one answer

- ⓐ use the lane that has least traffic
- ⓑ keep to the left lane unless overtaking
- ⓒ overtake on the side that is clearest
- ⓓ try to keep above 50 mph to prevent congestion

Question 18

On a three-lane motorway why should you normally ride in the left lane?

Mark one answer

- ⓐ The left lane is only for lorries and motorcycles
- ⓑ The left lane should only be used by smaller vehicles
- ⓒ The lanes on the right are for overtaking
- ⓓ Motorcycles are not allowed in the far right lane

Question 19

You are going at 70 mph on a three-lane motorway. There is no traffic ahead. Which lane should you use?

Mark one answer

ⓐ Any lane
ⓑ Middle lane
ⓒ Right lane
ⓓ Left lane

Question 20

The left-hand lane on a three-lane motorway is for use by

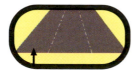

Mark one answer

ⓐ any vehicle
ⓑ large vehicles only
ⓒ emergency vehicles only
ⓓ slow vehicles only

Question 21

The left-hand lane of a motorway should be used for

Mark one answer

ⓐ breakdowns and emergencies only
ⓑ overtaking slower traffic in the other lanes
ⓒ slow vehicles only
ⓓ normal driving

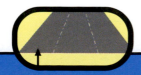

Question 22

What is the right hand-lane used for on a three-lane motorway?

Mark one answer

ⓐ Emergency vehicles only
ⓑ Overtaking
ⓒ Vehicles towing trailers
ⓓ Coaches only

Question 23

Which of these IS NOT allowed to travel in the right-hand lane of a three-lane motorway?

Mark one answer

ⓐ A small delivery van
ⓑ A motorcycle
ⓒ A vehicle towing a trailer
ⓓ A motorcycle and side-car

Question 24

For what reason may you use the right-hand lane of a motorway?

Mark one answer

ⓐ For keeping out of the way of lorries
ⓑ For driving at more than 70 mph
ⓒ For turning right
ⓓ For overtaking other vehicles

Question 25

On motorways you should never overtake on the left UNLESS

Mark one answer

ⓐ you can see well ahead that the hard shoulder is clear

ⓑ the traffic in the right-hand lane is signalling right

ⓒ you warn drivers behind by signalling left

ⓓ there is a queue of traffic to your right that is moving more slowly

Question 26

On a motorway you may ONLY stop on the hard shoulder

Mark one answer

ⓐ in an emergency

ⓑ If you feel tired and need to rest

ⓒ if you accidentally go past the exit that you wanted to take

ⓓ to pick up a hitchhiker

Question 27

You are travelling on a motorway. You decide you need a rest. You should

Mark two answers

ⓐ stop on the hard shoulder

ⓑ go to a service area

ⓒ park on the slip road

ⓓ park on the central reservation

ⓔ leave at the next exit

Question 28

You are driving on a motorway. The car ahead shows its hazard lights for a short time. This tells you that

Mark one answer

ⓐ the driver wants you to overtake

ⓑ the other car is going to change lanes

ⓒ traffic ahead is slowing or stopping suddenly

ⓓ there is a police speed check ahead

Question 29

You are driving on a motorway. You have to slow down quickly due to a hazard. You should

Mark one answer

ⓐ switch on your hazard lights

ⓑ switch on your headlights

ⓒ sound your horn

ⓓ flash your headlights

Question 30

You break down on a motorway. You need to call for help. Why may it be better to use an emergency roadside telephone rather than a mobile phone?

Mark one answer

ⓐ It connects you to a local garage

ⓑ Using a mobile phone will distract other drivers

ⓒ It allows easy location by the emergency services

ⓓ Mobile phones do not work on motorways

Question 31

Your vehicle breaks down on the hard shoulder of a motorway. You decide to use your mobile phone to call for help. You should

Mark one answer

ⓐ stand at the rear of the vehicle while making the call

ⓑ try to repair the vehicle yourself

ⓒ get out of the vehicle by the right hand door

ⓓ check your location from the marker posts on the left

Question 32

You get a puncture on the motorway. You manage to get your vehicle onto the hard shoulder. You should

Mark one answer

ⓐ change the wheel yourself immediately

ⓑ use the emergency telephone and call for assistance

ⓒ try to wave down another vehicle for help

ⓓ only change the wheel if you have a passenger to help you

Question 33

The emergency telephones on a motorway are connected to the

Mark one answer

ⓐ ambulance service

ⓑ police control

ⓒ fire brigade

ⓓ breakdown service

Question 34

How should you use the emergency telephone on a motorway?

Mark one answer

ⓐ Stay close to the carriageway

ⓑ Face the oncoming traffic

ⓒ Keep your back to the traffic

ⓓ Stand on the hard shoulder

Question 35

What should you use the hard shoulder of a motorway for?

Mark one answer

ⓐ Stopping in an emergency
ⓑ Leaving the motorway
ⓒ Stopping when you are tired
ⓓ Joining the motorway

Question 36

After a breakdown you need to rejoin the main carriageway of a motorway from the hard shoulder. You should

Mark one answer

ⓐ move out onto the carriageway then build up your speed
ⓑ move out onto the carriageway using your hazard lights
ⓒ gain speed on the hard shoulder before moving out onto the carriageway
ⓓ wait on the hard shoulder until someone flashes their headlights at you

Question 37

A crawler lane on a motorway is found

Mark one answer

ⓐ on a steep gradient
ⓑ before a service area
ⓒ before a junction
ⓓ along the hard shoulder

Question 38

Your vehicle has broken down on a motorway. You are not able to stop on the hard shoulder. What should you do?

Mark one answer

ⓐ Switch on your hazard warning lights
ⓑ Stop following traffic and ask for help
ⓒ Attempt to repair your vehicle quickly
ⓓ Stand behind your vehicle to warn others

Question 39

When may you stop on a motorway?

Mark three answers

ⓐ If you have to read a map
ⓑ When you are tired and need a rest
ⓒ If red lights show above every lane
ⓓ When told to by the police
ⓔ If your mobile phone rings
ⓕ In an emergency or a breakdown

Question 40

You are allowed to stop on a motorway when you

Mark one answer

- a need to walk and get fresh air
- b wish to pick up hitchhikers
- c are told to do so by flashing red lights
- d need to use a mobile telephone

Question 41

You are on a motorway. There are red flashing lights above every lane. You must

Mark one answer

- a pull onto the hard shoulder
- b slow down and watch for further signals
- c leave at the next exit
- d stop and wait

Question 42

You are in the right-hand lane on a motorway. You see these overhead signs. This means

Mark one answer

- a move to the left and reduce your speed to 50 mph
- b there are roadworks 50 metres (55 yards) ahead
- c use the hard shoulder until you have passed the hazard
- d leave the motorway at the next exit

Question 43

When going through a contraflow system on a motorway you should

Mark one answer

- a ensure that you do not exceed 30 mph
- b keep a good distance from the vehicle ahead
- c switch lanes to keep the traffic flowing
- d stay close to the vehicle ahead to reduce queues

Question 44

You are intending to leave the motorway at the next exit. Before you reach the exit you should normally position your vehicle

Mark one answer

- a in the middle lane
- b in the left-hand lane
- c on the hard shoulder
- d in any lane

Question 45

What do these motorway signs show?

Mark one answer

ⓐ They are countdown markers to a bridge

ⓑ They are distance markers to the next telephone

ⓒ They are countdown markers to the next exit

ⓓ They warn of a police control ahead

Question 46

You are driving on a motorway. By mistake, you go past the exit that you wanted to take. You should

Mark one answer

ⓐ carefully reverse on the hard shoulder

ⓑ carry on to the next exit

ⓒ carefully reverse in the left-hand lane

ⓓ make a U-turn at the next gap in the central reservation

Question 47

On a motorway the amber reflective studs can be found between

Mark one answer

ⓐ the hard shoulder and the carriageway

ⓑ the acceleration lane and the carriageway

ⓒ the central reservation and the carriageway

ⓓ each pair of the lanes

Question 48

What colour are the reflective studs between the lanes on a motorway?

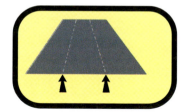

Mark one answer

ⓐ Green

ⓑ Amber

ⓒ White

ⓓ Red

Question 49

You are on a three-lane motorway. There are red reflective studs on your left and white ones to your right. Where are you?

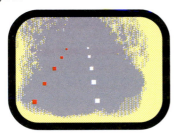

Mark one answer

- a) In the right-hand lane
- b) In the middle lane
- c) On the hard shoulder
- d) In the left-hand lane

Question 50

What colour are the reflective studs between a motorway and its slip road?

Mark one answer

- a) Amber
- b) White
- c) Green
- d) Red

Question 51

You are on a motorway. What colour are the reflective studs on the left of the carriageway?

Mark one answer

- a) Green
- b) Red
- c) White
- d) Amber

Question 52

You have broken down on a motorway. To find the nearest emergency telephone you should always walk

Mark one answer

- a) with the traffic flow
- b) facing oncoming traffic
- c) in the direction shown on the marker posts
- d) in the direction of the nearest exit

Question 53

You are travelling along the left lane of a three-lane motorway. Traffic is joining from a slip road. You should

Mark one answer

- ⓐ race the other vehicles
- ⓑ move to another lane
- ⓒ maintain a steady speed
- ⓓ switch on your hazard flashers

Question 54

You are on a three-lane motorway towing a trailer. You may use the right hand lane when

Mark one answer

- ⓐ there are lane closures
- ⓑ there is slow-moving traffic
- ⓒ you can maintain a high speed
- ⓓ large vehicles are in the left and centre lanes

Answers and explanations

Q001 c
Q002 a,d,e,f
Q003 a,d,e,f
Q004 a
Q005 a
Q006 d Check oil and windscreen washer levels and also check the tyres. Plan your rest stops.
Q007 d
Q008 c You need to build up your speed to that of the traffic already on the motorway so you can ease into a gap in the flow of traffic.
Q009 a The slip road gives you time and space to adjust your speed to that of the traffic on the motorway.
Q010 d
Q011 c
Q012 d
Q013 d Speed limits may be altered due to weather conditions. Look out for signs on the central reserve or above your lane.
Q014 c When towing a trailer strong winds can affect stability.
Q015 c
Q016 a The other lanes should be used for overtaking.

Answers and explanations

Q017 b

Q018 c

Q019 d You should always use the left-hand lane for normal driving.

Q020 a Strictly speaking, any vehicle which is allowed on a motorway.

Q021 d

Q022 b

Q023 c

Q024 d

Q025 d

Q026 a

Q027 b,e

Q028 c

Q029 a

Q030 c

Q031 d

Q032 b It is dangerous to attempt to change the wheel yourself. Try to keep as far from the carriageway as possible whilst waiting for assistance.

Q033 b

Q034 b

Q035 a You may only stop on the hard shoulder in an emergency.

Q036 c

Q037 a

Q038 a

Q039 c,d,f Service areas are not officially part of the motorway.

Q040 c

Q041 d

Q042 a

Q043 b In these circumstances there may also be a speed limit – keep to it.

Q044 b

Q045 c

Q046 b

Q047 c

Q048 c

Q049 d

Q050 c

Q051 b

Q052 c

Q053 b

Q054 a

Driving Theory
Test
Questions
2000/2001

Rules of the Road

We won't fail you

Question 1

You are riding slowly in a town centre. Before turning left you should glance over your left shoulder to

Mark one answer

- a. check for cyclists
- b. help keep your balance
- c. look for traffic signs
- d. check for potholes

Question 2

You may drive over a footpath

Mark one answer

- a. to overtake slow-moving traffic
- b. when the pavement is very wide
- c. if no pedestrians are near
- d. to get into a property

Question 3

What is the meaning of this sign?

Mark one answer

- a. Local speed limit applies
- b. No waiting on the carriageway
- c. National speed limit applies
- d. No entry to vehicular traffic

Question 4

What is the national speed limit on a single carriageway road for cars and motorcycles?

Mark one answer

- a. 70 mph
- b. 60 mph
- c. 50 mph
- d. 30 mph

Question 5

What is the national speed limit for cars and motorcycles on a dual carriageway?

Mark one answer

- a. 30 mph
- b. 50 mph
- c. 60 mph
- d. 70 mph

Question 6

A single carriageway road has this sign. What is the maximum permitted speed for a car towing a trailer?

Mark one answer

- a. 30 mph
- b. 40 mph
- c. 50 mph
- d. 60 mph

Question 7

You are on a road that has no traffic signs. There are street lights. What is the speed limit?

Mark one answer

[a] 20 mph
[b] 30 mph
[c] 40 mph
[d] 60 mph

Question 8

There are no speed limit signs on the road. How is a 30 mph limit indicated?

Mark one answer

[a] By hazard warning lines
[b] By street lighting
[c] By pedestrian islands
[d] By double or single yellow lines

Question 9

Where you see street lights but no speed limit signs the limit is usually

Mark one answer

[a] 30 mph
[b] 40 mph
[c] 50 mph
[d] 60 mph

Question 10

You are towing a small caravan on a dual carriageway. You must not exceed

Mark one answer

[a] 50 mph
[b] 40 mph
[c] 70 mph
[d] 60 mph

Question 11

What does this sign mean?

Mark one answer

[a] Minimum speed 30 mph
[b] End of maximum speed
[c] End of minimum speed
[d] Maximum speed 30 mph

Question 12

You are going along a street with parked vehicles on the left-hand side. For which THREE reasons should you keep your speed down?

Mark three answers

- ⓐ So that oncoming traffic can see you more clearly
- ⓑ You may set off car alarms
- ⓒ Vehicles may be pulling out
- ⓓ Drivers' doors may open
- ⓔ Children may run out from between the vehicles

Question 13

You meet an obstruction on your side of the road. You should

Mark one answer

- ⓐ carry on, you have priority
- ⓑ give way to oncoming traffic
- ⓒ wave oncoming vehicles through
- ⓓ accelerate to get past first

Question 14

There is a tractor ahead of you. You wish to overtake but you are NOT sure if it is safe to do so. You should

Mark one answer

- ⓐ follow another overtaking vehicle through
- ⓑ sound your horn to the slow vehicle to pull over
- ⓒ speed through but flash your lights to oncoming traffic
- ⓓ not overtake if you are in doubt

Question 15

Which three of the following are most likely to take an unusual course at roundabouts?

Mark three answers

- ⓐ Horse riders
- ⓑ Milk floats
- ⓒ Delivery vans
- ⓓ Long vehicles
- ⓔ Estate cars
- ⓕ Cyclists

Question 16

You are leaving your vehicle parked on a road. When may you leave the engine running?

Mark one answer

ⓐ If you will be parked for less than five minutes

ⓑ If the battery is flat

ⓒ When in a 20 mph zone

ⓓ Not on any occasion

Question 17

In which FOUR places must you NOT park or wait?

Mark four answers

ⓐ On a dual carriageway

ⓑ At a bus stop

ⓒ On the slope of a hill

ⓓ Opposite a traffic island

ⓔ In front of someone else's drive

ⓕ On the brow of a hill

Question 18

What is the nearest you may park your vehicle to a junction?

Mark one answer

ⓐ 10 metres (32 feet)

ⓑ 12 metres (39 feet)

ⓒ 15 metres (49 feet)

ⓓ 20 metres (66 feet)

Question 19

You are finding it difficult to find a parking place in a busy town. You can see there is space on the zigzag lines of a zebra crossing. Can you park there?

Mark one answer

ⓐ No, unless you stay with your car

ⓑ Yes, in order to drop off a passenger

ⓒ Yes, if you do not block people from crossing

ⓓ No, not in any circumstances

Question 20

In which TWO places must you NOT park?

Mark two answers

ⓐ Near a school entrance

ⓑ Near a police station

ⓒ In a side road

ⓓ At a bus stop

ⓔ In a one-way street

Question 21

In which THREE places must you NOT park your vehicle?

Mark three answers

ⓐ Near the brow of a hill

ⓑ At or near a bus stop

ⓒ Where there is no pavement

ⓓ Within 10 metres (32 feet) of a junction

ⓔ On a 40 mph road

Question 22

On a clearway you must not stop

Mark one answer

ⓐ at any time
ⓑ when it is busy
ⓒ in the rush hour
ⓓ during daylight hours

Question 23

You are driving on an urban clearway.
You may stop only to

Mark one answer

ⓐ set down and pick up passengers
ⓑ use a mobile telephone
ⓒ ask for directions
ⓓ load or unload goods

Question 24

You want to park and you see this sign.
On the days and times shown you should

Mark one answer

ⓐ park in a bay and not pay
ⓑ park on yellow lines and pay
ⓒ park on yellow lines and not pay
ⓓ park in a bay and pay

Question 25

What is the meaning of this sign?

Mark one answer

ⓐ No entry
ⓑ Waiting restrictions
ⓒ National speed limit
ⓓ School-crossing patrol

Question 26

What MUST you have to park in a
disabled space?

Mark one answer

ⓐ An orange badge
ⓑ A wheelchair
ⓒ An advanced driver certificate
ⓓ A modified vehicle

Question 27

You are looking for somewhere to park your vehicle. The area is full EXCEPT for spaces marked 'disabled use'. You can

Mark one answer

ⓐ use these spaces when elsewhere is full

ⓑ park if you stay with your vehicle

ⓒ use these spaces, disabled or not

ⓓ not park there unless permitted

Question 28

Your vehicle is parked on the road at night. When must you use sidelights?

Mark one answer

ⓐ Where there are continuous white lines in the middle of the road

ⓑ Where the speed limit exceeds 30 mph

ⓒ Where you are facing oncoming traffic

ⓓ Where you are near a bus stop

Question 29

You park overnight on a road with a 40 mph speed limit. You should

Mark one answer

ⓐ park facing the traffic

ⓑ park with sidelights on

ⓒ park with dipped headlights on

ⓓ park near a street light

Question 30

You can park on the right-hand side of a road at night

Mark one answer

ⓐ in a one-way street

ⓑ with your sidelights on

ⓒ more than 10 metres (32 feet) from a junction

ⓓ under a lamp-post

Question 31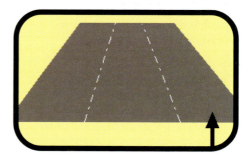

On a three-lane dual carriageway the right-hand lane can be used for

Mark one answer

ⓐ overtaking only, never turning right

ⓑ overtaking or turning right

ⓒ fast-moving traffic only

ⓓ turning right only, never overtaking

Question 32

You are driving at night with full beam headlights on. A vehicle is overtaking you. You should dip your lights

Mark one answer

- (a) some time after the vehicle has passed you
- (b) before the vehicle starts to pass you
- (c) only if the other driver dips his headlights
- (d) as soon as the vehicle passes you

Question 33

You are riding on a busy dual carriageway. When changing lanes you should

Mark one answer

- (a) rely totally on mirrors
- (b) always increase your speed
- (c) signal so others will give way
- (d) use mirrors and shoulder checks

Question 34

You are on a two-lane dual carriageway. For which TWO of the following would you use the right-hand lane?

Mark two answers

- (a) Turning right
- (b) Normal progress
- (c) Staying at the minimum allowed speed
- (d) Constant high speed
- (e) Overtaking slower traffic
- (f) Mending punctures

Question 35

You are in the right-hand lane of a dual carriageway. You see signs showing that the right lane is closed 800 yards ahead. You should

Mark one answer

- (a) keep in that lane until you reach the queue
- (b) move to the left immediately
- (c) wait and see which lane is moving faster
- (d) move to the left in good time

Question 36

You are entering an area of roadworks. There is a temporary speed limit displayed. You must

Mark one answer

- (a) not exceed the speed limit
- (b) obey the limit only during rush hour
- (c) accept the speed limit as advisable
- (d) obey the limit except for overnight

Question 37

While driving, you approach roadworks. You see a temporary maximum speed limit sign. You must

Mark one answer

ⓐ comply with the sign during the working day

ⓑ comply with the sign at all times

ⓒ comply with the sign when the lanes are narrow

ⓓ comply with the sign during the hours of darkness

Question 38

You may drive a motor car in this bus lane

Mark one answer

ⓐ outside its operation hours

ⓑ to get to the front of a traffic queue

ⓒ at no times at all

ⓓ to overtake slow-moving traffic

Question 39

As a car driver which THREE lanes are you NOT normally allowed to use?

Mark three answers

ⓐ Crawler lane

ⓑ Bus lane

ⓒ Overtaking lane

ⓓ Acceleration lane

ⓔ Cycle lane

ⓕ Tram lane

Question 40

You are driving on a road that has a cycle lane. The lane is marked by a broken white line. This means that

Mark two answers

ⓐ you should not drive in the lane unless it is unavoidable

ⓑ you should not park in the lane unless it is unavoidable

ⓒ you can drive in the lane at any time

ⓓ the lane must be used by motorcyclists in heavy traffic

Question 41

You are driving along a road that has a cycle lane. The lane is marked by a solid white line. This means that during its period of operation

Mark one answer

ⓐ the lane may be used for parking your car

ⓑ you may drive in that lane at any time

ⓒ the lane may be used when necessary

ⓓ you must not drive in that lane

Question 42

A cycle lane is marked by a solid white line. You must not drive or park in it

Mark one answer

ⓐ at any time

ⓑ during the rush hour

ⓒ if a cyclist is using it

ⓓ during its period of operation

Question 43

As a motorcycle rider which TWO lanes must you NOT use?

Mark two answers

ⓐ Crawler lane

ⓑ Overtaking lane

ⓒ Acceleration lane

ⓓ Cycle lane

ⓔ Tram lane

Question 44

You are approaching a busy junction. There are several lanes with road markings. At the last moment you realise that you are in the wrong lane. You should

Mark one answer

ⓐ continue in that lane

ⓑ force your way across

ⓒ stop until the area has cleared

ⓓ use clear arm signals to cut across

Question 45

Where may you overtake on a one-way street?

Mark one answer

ⓐ Only on the left-hand side

ⓑ Overtaking is not allowed

ⓒ Only on the right-hand side

ⓓ Either on the right or the left

Question 46

You are going along a single-track road with passing places only on the right. The driver behind wishes to overtake. You should

Mark one answer

ⓐ speed up to get away from the following driver

ⓑ switch on your hazard warning lights

ⓒ wait opposite a passing place on your right

ⓓ pull into a passing place on your right

Question 47

You are on a road that is only wide enough for one vehicle. There is a car coming towards you. Which TWO of these would be correct?

Mark two answers

ⓐ Pull into a passing place on your right
ⓑ Force the other driver to reverse
ⓒ Pull into a passing place if your vehicle is wider
ⓓ Pull into a passing place on your left
ⓔ Wait opposite a passing place on your right
ⓕ Wait opposite a passing place on your left

Question 48

Signals are normally given by direction indicators and

Mark one answer

ⓐ brake lights
ⓑ side lights
ⓒ fog lights
ⓓ interior lights

Question 49

When going straight ahead at a roundabout you should

Mark one answer

ⓐ indicate left before leaving the roundabout
ⓑ not indicate at any time
ⓒ indicate right when approaching the roundabout
ⓓ indicate left when approaching the roundabout

Question 50

Which vehicle might have to use a different course to normal at roundabouts?

Mark one answer

ⓐ Sports car
ⓑ Van
ⓒ Estate car
ⓓ Long vehicle

Question 51

You are going straight ahead at a roundabout. How should you signal?

Mark one answer

ⓐ Signal right on the approach and then left to leave the roundabout
ⓑ Signal left as you leave the roundabout
ⓒ Signal left on the approach to the roundabout and keep the signal on until you leave
ⓓ Signal left just after you pass the exit before the one you will take

Question 52

You are turning right at a large roundabout. Just before you leave the roundabout you should

Mark one answer

- (a) take a 'lifesaver' glance over your left shoulder
- (b) take a 'lifesaver' glance over your right shoulder
- (c) put on your right indicator
- (d) cancel the left indicator

Question 53

At a crossroads there are no signs or road markings. Two vehicles approach. Which has priority?

Mark one answer

- (a) Neither vehicle
- (b) The vehicle travelling the fastest
- (c) The vehicle on the widest road
- (d) Vehicles approaching from the right

Question 54

Who has priority at an unmarked crossroads?

Mark one answer

- (a) The larger vehicle
- (b) No one has priority
- (c) The faster vehicle
- (d) The smaller vehicle

Question 55

When filtering through slow-moving or stationary traffic you should

Mark three answers

- (a) watch for hidden vehicles emerging from side roads
- (b) continually use your horn as a warning
- (c) look for vehicles changing course suddenly
- (d) always ride with your hazard lights on
- (e) stand up on the footrests for a good view ahead
- (f) Look for pedestrians walking between vehicles

Question 56

You are intending to turn right at a crossroads. An oncoming driver is also turning right. It will normally be safer to

Mark one answer

- (a) keep the other vehicle to your RIGHT and turn behind it (offside to offside)
- (b) keep the other vehicle to your LEFT and turn in front of it (nearside to nearside)
- (c) carry on and turn at the next junction instead
- (d) hold back and wait for the other driver to turn first

Question 57

You are both turning right at these crossroads. It is safer to keep the car to your right so you can

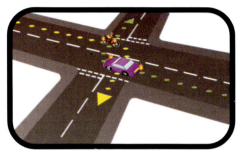

Mark one answer

- ⓐ see approaching traffic
- ⓑ keep close to the kerb
- ⓒ keep clear of following traffic
- ⓓ make oncoming vehicles stop

Question 58

The dual carriageway you are turning right onto has a narrow central reserve. You should

Mark one answer

- ⓐ proceed to central reserve and wait
- ⓑ wait until the road is clear in both directions
- ⓒ stop in the first lane so that other vehicles give way
- ⓓ emerge slightly to show your intentions

Question 59

While driving, you intend to turn left into a minor road. On the approach you should

Mark one answer

- ⓐ keep just left of the middle of the road
- ⓑ keep in the middle of the road
- ⓒ swing out wide just before turning
- ⓓ keep well to the left of the road

Question 60

You may only enter a box junction when

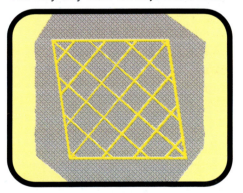

Mark one answer

- ⓐ there are less than two vehicles in front of you
- ⓑ the traffic lights show green
- ⓒ your exit road is clear
- ⓓ you need to turn left

Question 61

You may wait in a yellow box junction when

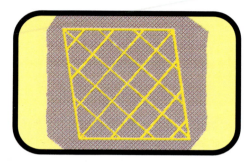

Mark one answer

- ⓐ oncoming traffic is preventing you from turning right
- ⓑ you are in a queue of traffic turning left
- ⓒ you are in a queue of traffic to go ahead
- ⓓ you are on a roundabout

Question 62

You want to turn right at a box junction. There is oncoming traffic. You should

Mark one answer

- ⓐ wait in the box junction if your exit is clear
- ⓑ wait before the junction until it is clear of all traffic
- ⓒ drive on: you cannot turn right at a box junction
- ⓓ drive slowly into the box junction when signalled by oncoming traffic

Question 63

On which THREE occasions MUST you stop your vehicle?

Mark three answers

- ⓐ When involved in an accident
- ⓑ At a red traffic light
- ⓒ When signalled to do so by a police officer
- ⓓ At a junction with double broken white lines
- ⓔ At a pelican crossing when the amber light is flashing and no pedestrians are crossing

Question 64

You MUST stop when signalled to do so by which THREE of these?

Mark three answers

- ⓐ A police officer
- ⓑ A pedestrian
- ⓒ A school-crossing patrol
- ⓓ A bus driver
- ⓔ A red traffic light

Question 65

At roadworks which of the following can control traffic flow?

Mark three answers

- ⓐ A STOP–GO board
- ⓑ Flashing amber lights
- ⓒ A policeman
- ⓓ Flashing red lights
- ⓔ Temporary traffic lights

Question 66

You are waiting at a level crossing. The red warning lights continue to flash after a train has passed by. What should you do?

Mark one answer

ⓐ Get out and investigate

ⓑ Telephone the signal operator

ⓒ Continue to wait

ⓓ Drive across carefully

Question 67

You are driving over a level crossing. The warning lights come on and a bell rings. What should you do?

Mark one answer

ⓐ Get everyone out of the vehicle immediately

ⓑ Stop and reverse back to clear the crossing

ⓒ Keep going and clear the crossing

ⓓ Stop immediately and use your hazard warning lights

Question 68

You are waiting at a level crossing. A train has passed but the lights keep flashing. You must

Mark one answer

ⓐ carry on waiting

ⓑ phone the signal operator

ⓒ edge over the stop line and look for trains

ⓓ park your vehicle and investigate

Question 69

You will see these markers when approaching

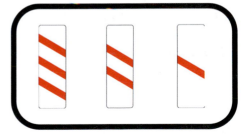

Mark one answer

ⓐ the end of a motorway

ⓑ a concealed level crossing

ⓒ a concealed speed limit sign

ⓓ the end of a dual carriageway

Question 70

Someone is waiting to cross at a zebra crossing. They are standing on the pavement. You should normally

Mark one answer

- ⓐ go on quickly before they step onto the crossing
- ⓑ stop before you reach the zigzag lines and let them cross
- ⓒ stop, let them cross, wait patiently
- ⓓ ignore them as they are still on the pavement

Question 71

At toucan crossings, apart from pedestrians you should be aware of

Mark one answer

- ⓐ emergency vehicles emerging
- ⓑ buses pulling out
- ⓒ trams crossing in front
- ⓓ cyclists riding across

Question 72

Who can use a toucan crossing?

Mark two answers

- ⓐ Trains
- ⓑ Cyclists
- ⓒ Buses
- ⓓ Pedestrians
- ⓔ Trams

Question 73

At a pelican crossing, what does a flashing amber light mean?

Mark one answer

- ⓐ You must not move off until the lights stop flashing
- ⓑ You must give way to pedestrians still on the crossing
- ⓒ You can move off, even if pedestrians are still on the crossing
- ⓓ You must stop because the lights are about to change to red

Question 74

You are waiting at a pelican crossing. The red light changes to flashing amber. This means you must

Mark one answer

- ⓐ wait for pedestrians on the crossing to clear
- ⓑ move off immediately without any hesitation
- ⓒ wait for the green light before moving off
- ⓓ get ready and go when the continuous amber light shows

Question 75

You are on a busy main road and find that you are travelling in the wrong direction. What should you do?

Mark one answer

a Turn into a side road on the right and reverse into the main road

b Make a U-turn in the main road

c Make a 'three-point' turn in the main road

d Turn round in a side road

Question 76

You may remove your seat belt when carrying out a manoeuvre that involves

Mark one answer

a reversing

b a hill start

c an emergency stop

d driving slowly

Question 77

You must not reverse

Mark one answer

a for longer than necessary

b for more than a car's length

c into a side road

d in a built-up area

Question 78

You are parked in a busy high street. What is the safest way to turn your vehicle around to go the opposite way?

Mark one answer

a Find a quiet side road to turn round in

b Drive into a side road and reverse into the main road

c Get someone to stop the traffic

d Do a U-turn

Question 79

When you are NOT sure that it is safe to reverse your vehicle you should

Mark one answer

a use your horn

b rev your engine

c get out and check

d reverse slowly

Question 80

When may you reverse from a side road into a main road?

Mark one answer

a Only if both roads are clear of traffic

b Not at any time

c At any time

d Only if the main road is clear of traffic

Question 81

You are reversing your vehicle into a side road. When would the greatest hazard to passing traffic occur?

Mark one answer

ⓐ After you've completed the manoeuvre
ⓑ Just before you actually begin to manoeuvre
ⓒ After you've entered the side road
ⓓ When the front of your vehicle swings out

Question 82

You want to tow a trailer with your motorcycle. Your engine must be more than

Mark one answer

ⓐ 50cc
ⓑ 125cc
ⓒ 525cc
ⓓ 1000cc

Question 83

What is the national speed limit on a single carriageway?

Mark one answer

ⓐ 40mph
ⓑ 50mph
ⓒ 60mph
ⓓ 70mph

Question 84

What does this sign mean?

Mark one answer

ⓐ No parking for solo motorcycles
ⓑ Parking for solo motorcycles
ⓒ Passing place for motorcycles
ⓓ Police motorcycles only

Question 85

Your motorcycle will be parked for a long time. You should

Mark three answers

ⓐ use the centre stand if fitted
ⓑ park on a wide pavement
ⓒ lean it against a wall
ⓓ switch off the fuel tap
ⓔ park where the ground is firm and level
ⓕ park with your lights on in daytime

Question 86

You are riding towards roadworks. The temporary traffic lights are at red. The road ahead is clear. What should you do?

Mark one answer

ⓐ Ride on with extreme caution
ⓑ Ride on at normal speed
ⓒ Carry on if approaching cars have stopped
ⓓ Wait for the green light

Question 87

You are travelling on a well-lit road at night in a built-up area. By using dipped headlights you will be able to

Mark one answer

ⓐ see further along the road
ⓑ go at a much faster speed
ⓒ switch to main beam quickly
ⓓ be easily seen by others

Question 88

When can you park on the left opposite these road markings?

Mark one answer

ⓐ If the line nearest to you is broken
ⓑ When there are no yellow lines
ⓒ To pick up or set down passengers
ⓓ During daylight hours only

Answers and explanations

Q001   a
Q002   d
Q003   c
Q004   b
Q005   d The national speed limit is 70 mph on a motorway or dual carriageway and 60 mph on two-way roads unless traffic signs denote anything different.
Q006   c
Q007   b If there are street lights, the speed limit is 30 mph unless a road sign states otherwise.
Q008   b
Q009   a If there is any difference there would be repeated signs on the light posts.
Q010   d
Q011   c
Q012   c,d,e
Q013   b
Q014   d
Q015   a,d,f
Q016   d
Q017   b,d,e,f
Q018   a
Q019   d It is illegal to park on the zigzag lines of a pedestrian crossing for any reason or at any time.

Answers and explanations

Q020 a,d

Q021 a,b,d

Q022 a

Q023 a

Q024 d

Q025 b

Q026 a

Q027 d

Q028 b

Q029 b

Q030 a

Q031 b

Q032 d If you dip your lights too early you may reduce your vision; too late and you may dazzle the driver who has overtaken.

Q033 d A shoulder check allows you to see a vehicle that may be in your blindspot.

Q034 a,e

Q035 d

Q036 a

Q037 b

Q038 a

Q039 b,e,f

Q040 a,b

Q041 d

Q042 d

Q043 d,e

Q044 a All the other actions suggested could be dangerous.

Q045 d

Q046 c

Q047 d,e

Q048 a When you press your brake pedal the brake lights come on, warning other vehicles behind.

Q049 a You should signal left just as you pass the exit before the one you want to take.

Q050 d

Q051 d This is correct for most roundabouts. Bear in mind that some roundabouts do not have an exit to the left, so the first exit is straight ahead.

Q052 a You need to check for vehicles in your left blind spot.

Q053 a You often find these on housing estates. Approach with caution and be prepared to give way.

Q054 b An unmarked crossroads has no road signs or road markings and no vehicle has priority even if one road is wider or busier than the other.

Answers and explanations

Q055 a,c,f

Q056 a

Q057 a

Q058 b Because the central reserve is narrow, you would partly block the road if you drove to the middle and had to wait.

Q059 d

Q060 c

Q061 a

Q062 a

Q063 a,b,c

'd' is wrong because although the double, broken white lines at a junction mean 'give way', you do not necessarily have to stop in order to do so. 'e' is wrong because you may drive on at a pelican crossing when the amber light is flashing if no pedestrians are crossing.

Q064 a,c,e

Note the word 'MUST' in the question, which is asking what the law says.

Q065 a,c,e

Q066 c You should wait for three minutes. If no further train passes you should telephone the signal operator.

Q067 c You are already on the crossing when the warning lights come on, so 'c' is correct.

Q068 a

Q069 b These countdown markers indicate the distance to the stop line at the concealed level crossing.

Q070 c Note the word 'normally'. You should give way if safe to do so.

Q071 d Cyclists are allowed to ride across toucan crossings, unlike other crossings where they must dismount.

Q072 b,d

Toucan crossings are shared by pedestrians and cyclists together.

Q073 b You may drive as soon as the crossing is clear and before the flashing amber light changes to green.

Q074 a

Q075 d It is illegal to reverse from a minor to a major road, so 'a' is wrong. 'b' and 'c' would be dangerous because the road is busy.

Q076 a

Answers and explanations

Q077 a

Q078 a

Q079 c

Q080 b

Q081 d Always remember to check all round just before steering and give way to any road users.

Q082 b

Q083 c

Q084 b

Q085 a,d,e

Q086 d

Q087 d

Q088 c

Driving Theory
Test
Questions
2000/2001

Road & Traffic Signs

BSM
We won't fail you

Question 1

You MUST obey signs giving orders. These signs are mostly in

Mark one answer

[a] green rectangles

[b] red triangles

[c] blue rectangles

[d] red circles

Question 2

Traffic signs giving orders are generally which shape?

Mark one answer

[a]

[b]

[c]

[d]

Question 3

Which type of sign tells you NOT to do something?

Mark one answer

[a]

[b]

[c]

[d]

Question 4

What does this sign mean?

Mark one answer

[a] Maximum speed limit with traffic calming

[b] Minimum speed limit with traffic calming

[c] '20 cars only' parking zone

[d] Only 20 cars allowed at any one time

Question 5

Which sign means no motor vehicles are allowed?

Mark one answer

[a]

[b]

[c]

[d]

Question 6

Which of these signs means no motor vehicles?

Mark one answer

ⓐ

ⓑ

ⓒ

ⓓ

Question 7

What does this sign mean?

Mark one answer

ⓐ New speed limit 20 mph

ⓑ No vehicles over 30 tonnes

ⓒ Minimum speed limit 30 mph

ⓓ End of 20 mph zone

Question 8

This traffic sign means there is

Mark one answer

ⓐ a compulsory maximum speed limit

ⓑ an advisory maximum speed limit

ⓒ a compulsory minimum speed limit

ⓓ an advised separation distance

Question 9

What does this sign mean?

Mark one answer

ⓐ No overtaking

ⓑ No motor vehicles

ⓒ Clearway (no stopping)

ⓓ Cars and motorcycles only

Question 10

What does this sign mean?

Mark one answer

- ⓐ No parking
- ⓑ No road markings
- ⓒ No through road
- ⓓ No entry

Question 11

What does this sign mean?

Mark one answer

- ⓐ Bend to the right
- ⓑ Road on the right closed
- ⓒ No traffic from the right
- ⓓ No right turn

Question 12

Which sign means 'no entry'?

Mark one answer

ⓐ   ⓑ

ⓒ   ⓓ

Question 13

What does this sign mean?

Mark one answer

- ⓐ Route for trams only
- ⓑ Route for buses only
- ⓒ Parking for buses only
- ⓓ Parking for trams only

Question 14

Which type of vehicle does this sign apply to?

Mark one answer

- [a] Wide vehicles
- [b] Long vehicles
- [c] High vehicles
- [d] Heavy vehicles

Question 15

Which sign means NO motor vehicles allowed?

Mark one answer

[a]

[b]

[c]

[d]

Question 16

What does this sign mean?

Mark one answer

- [a] You have priority
- [b] No motor vehicles
- [c] Two-way traffic
- [d] No overtaking

Question 17

What does this sign mean?

Mark one answer

- [a] Keep in one lane
- [b] Give way to oncoming traffic
- [c] Do not overtake
- [d] Form two lanes

Question 18

Which sign means no overtaking?

Mark one answer

ⓐ

ⓑ

ⓒ

ⓓ

Question 19

What does this sign mean?

Mark one answer

ⓐ Waiting restrictions apply
ⓑ Waiting permitted
ⓒ National speed limit applies
ⓓ Clearway (no stopping)

Question 20

What does this sign mean?

Mark one answer

ⓐ You can park on the days and times shown
ⓑ No parking on the days and times shown
ⓒ No parking at all from Monday to Friday
ⓓ You can park at any time; the urban clearway ends

Question 21

What does this sign mean?

Mark one answer

ⓐ End of restricted speed area
ⓑ End of restricted parking area
ⓒ End of clearway
ⓓ End of cycle route

Question 22

Which sign means 'no stopping'?

Mark one answer

(a)

(b)

(c)

(d)

Question 23

What does this sign mean?

Mark one answer

(a) Roundabout

(b) Crossroads

(c) No stopping

(d) No entry

Question 24

You see this sign ahead. It means

Mark one answer

(a) national speed limit applies

(b) waiting restrictions apply

(c) no stopping

(d) no entry

Question 25

What does this sign mean?

Mark one answer

(a) Distance to parking place ahead

(b) Distance to public telephone ahead

(c) Distance to public house ahead

(d) Distance to passing place ahead

Question 26

What does this sign mean?

Mark one answer

ⓐ Vehicles may not park on the verge or footway

ⓑ Vehicles may park on the left-hand side of the road only

ⓒ Vehicles may park fully on the verge or footway

ⓓ Vehicles may park on the right-hand side of the road only

Question 27

What does this traffic sign mean?

Mark one answer

ⓐ No overtaking allowed

ⓑ Give priority to oncoming traffic

ⓒ Two-way traffic

ⓓ One-way traffic only

Question 28

What is the meaning of this traffic sign?

Mark one answer

ⓐ End of two-way road

ⓑ Give priority to vehicles coming towards you

ⓒ You have priority over vehicles coming towards you

ⓓ Bus lane ahead

Question 29

Which sign means 'traffic has priority over oncoming vehicles'?

Mark one answer

ⓐ

ⓑ

ⓒ

ⓓ

Question 30

What MUST you do when you see this sign?

Mark one answer

- a) Stop, ONLY if traffic is approaching
- b) Stop, even if the road is clear
- c) Stop, ONLY if children are waiting to cross
- d) Stop, ONLY if a red light is showing

Question 31

What does this sign mean?

Mark one answer

- a) No overtaking
- b) You are entering a one-way street
- c) Two-way traffic ahead
- d) You have priority over vehicles from the opposite direction

Question 32

What shape is a STOP sign at a junction?

Mark one answer

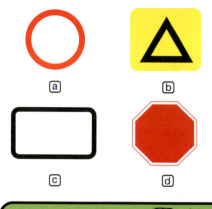

Question 33

At a junction you see this sign partly covered by snow. What does it mean?

Mark one answer

- a) Crossroads
- b) Give way
- c) Stop
- d) Turn right

Question 34

Which shape is used for a GIVE WAY sign?

Mark one answer

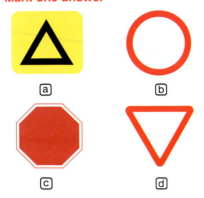

ⓐ   ⓑ

ⓒ   ⓓ

Question 36

Which of these signs means turn left ahead?

Mark one answer

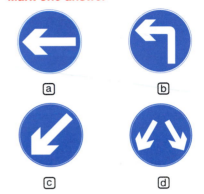

ⓐ   ⓑ

ⓒ   ⓓ

Question 35

What does this sign mean?

Mark one answer

ⓐ Service area 30 miles ahead
ⓑ Maximum speed 30 mph
ⓒ Minimum speed 30 mph
ⓓ Lay-by 30 miles ahead

Question 37

At a mini-roundabout you should

Mark one answer

ⓐ give way to traffic from the right
ⓑ give way to traffic from the left
ⓒ give way to traffic from the other way
ⓓ stop even when clear

Question 38

What does this sign mean?

Mark one answer

- a) Buses turning
- b) Ring road
- c) Mini roundabout
- d) Keep right

Question 39

What does this sign mean?

Mark one answer

- a) Give way to oncoming vehicles
- b) Approaching traffic passes you on both sides
- c) Turn off at the next available junction
- d) Pass either side to get to the same destination

Question 40

What does this sign mean?

Mark one answer

- a) Route for trams
- b) Give way to trams
- c) Route for buses
- d) Give way to buses

Question 41

What does a circular traffic sign with a blue background do?

Mark one answer

- a) Give warning of a motorway ahead
- b) Give directions to a car park
- c) Give motorway information
- d) Give an instruction

Question 42

Which of these signs means that you are entering a one-way street?

Mark one answer

Question 43

Where would you see a contraflow bus and cycle lane?

Mark one answer

- ⓐ On a dual carriageway
- ⓑ On a roundabout
- ⓒ On an urban motorway
- ⓓ On a one-way street

Question 44

What does this sign mean?

Mark one answer

- ⓐ Bus station on the right
- ⓑ Contraflow bus lane
- ⓒ With-flow bus lane
- ⓓ Give way to buses

Question 45

What does this sign mean?

Mark one answer

- ⓐ With-flow bus and cycle lane
- ⓑ Contraflow bus and cycle lane
- ⓒ No buses and cycles allowed
- ⓓ No waiting for buses and cycles

Question 46

What does a sign with a brown background show?

Mark one answer

- ⓐ Tourist directions
- ⓑ Primary roads
- ⓒ Motorway routes
- ⓓ Minor routes

Question 47

This sign means

Mark one answer

- ⓐ tourist attraction
- ⓑ beware of trains
- ⓒ level crossing
- ⓓ beware of trams

Question 48

What are triangular signs for?

Mark one answer

- a To give warnings
- b To give information
- c To give orders
- d To give directions

Question 50

What does this sign mean?

Mark one answer

- a Multi-exit roundabout
- b Risk of ice
- c Six roads converge
- d Place of historical interest

Question 49

What does this sign mean?

Mark one answer

- a Turn left ahead
- b T-junction
- c No through road
- d Give way

Question 51

What does this sign mean?

Mark one answer

- a Crossroads
- b Level crossing with gate
- c Level crossing without gate
- d Ahead only

Question 52

What does this sign mean?

Mark one answer

- a) Ring road
- b) Mini-roundabout
- c) No vehicles
- d) Roundabout

Question 53

Which FOUR of these would be indicated by a triangular road sign?

Mark four answers

- a) Road narrows
- b) Ahead only
- c) Low bridge
- d) Minimum speed
- e) Children crossing
- f) T-junction

Question 54

What does this sign mean?

Mark one answer

- a) Cyclists must dismount
- b) Cycles are not allowed
- c) Cycle route ahead
- d) Cycle in single file

Question 55

Which sign means that pedestrians may be walking along the road?

Mark one answer

a)

b)

c)

d)

Question 56

Which of these signs warn you of a pedestrian crossing?

Mark one answer

a	b
c	d

Question 57

What does this sign mean?

Mark one answer

a No footpath ahead
b Pedestrians only ahead
c Pedestrian-crossing ahead
d School-crossing ahead

Question 58

What does this sign mean?

Mark one answer

a School-crossing patrol
b No pedestrians allowed
c Pedestrian zone – no vehicles
d Pedestrian-crossing ahead

Question 59

Which of these signs means there is a double bend ahead?

Mark one answer

a	b

c	d

Question 60

What does this sign mean?

Mark one answer

- ⓐ Wait at the barriers
- ⓑ Wait at the crossroads
- ⓒ Give way to trams
- ⓓ Give way to farm vehicles

Question 61

What does this sign mean?

Mark one answer

- ⓐ Humpback bridge
- ⓑ Humps in the road
- ⓒ Entrance to tunnel
- ⓓ Soft verges

Question 62

What does this sign mean?

Mark one answer

- ⓐ Low bridge ahead
- ⓑ Tunnel ahead
- ⓒ Ancient monument ahead
- ⓓ Accident black-spot ahead

Question 63

What does this sign mean?

Mark one answer

- ⓐ Two-way traffic straight ahead
- ⓑ Two-way traffic crossing a one-way street
- ⓒ Two-way traffic over a bridge
- ⓓ Two-way traffic crosses a two-way road

Question 64

Which sign means 'two-way traffic crosses a one-way road'?

Mark one answer

ⓐ

ⓑ

ⓒ

ⓓ

Question 65

Which of these signs means the end of a dual carriageway?

Mark one answer

ⓐ

ⓑ

ⓒ

ⓓ

Question 66

What does this sign mean?

Mark one answer

ⓐ End of dual carriageway

ⓑ Tall bridge

ⓒ Road narrows

ⓓ End of narrow bridge

Question 67

What does this sign mean?

Mark one answer

ⓐ Two-way traffic ahead across a one-way street

ⓑ Traffic approaching you has priority

ⓒ Two-way traffic straight ahead

ⓓ Motorway contraflow system ahead

Question 68

What does this sign mean?

Mark one answer

- ⓐ Crosswinds
- ⓑ Road noise
- ⓒ Airport
- ⓓ Adverse camber

Question 69

What does this traffic sign mean?

Mark one answer

- ⓐ Slippery road ahead
- ⓑ Tyres liable to punctures ahead
- ⓒ Danger ahead
- ⓓ Service area ahead

Question 70

You are about to overtake when you see this sign. You should

Mark one answer

- ⓐ overtake the other driver as quickly as possible
- ⓑ move to the right to get a better view
- ⓒ switch your headlights on before overtaking
- ⓓ hold back until you can see clearly ahead

Question 71

What does this sign mean?

Mark one answer

- ⓐ Level crossing with gate or barrier
- ⓑ Gated road ahead
- ⓒ Level crossing without gate or barrier
- ⓓ Cattle grid ahead

Question 72

What does this sign mean?

Mark one answer

- ⓐ No trams ahead
- ⓑ Oncoming trams
- ⓒ Trams crossing ahead
- ⓓ Trams only

Question 74

What does this sign mean?

Mark one answer

- ⓐ Quayside or river bank
- ⓑ Steep hill downwards
- ⓒ Slippery road
- ⓓ Road liable to flooding

Question 73

What does this sign mean?

Mark one answer

- ⓐ Adverse camber
- ⓑ Steep hill downwards
- ⓒ Uneven road
- ⓓ Steep hill upwards

Question 75

What does this sign mean?

Mark one answer

- ⓐ Uneven road surface
- ⓑ Bridge over the road
- ⓒ Road ahead ends
- ⓓ Water across the road

Question 76

What does this sign mean?

Mark one answer

ⓐ Humpback bridge
ⓑ Traffic-calming hump
ⓒ Low bridge
ⓓ Uneven road

Question 77

What does this sign mean?

Mark one answer

ⓐ Turn left for parking area
ⓑ No through road on the left
ⓒ No entry for traffic turning left
ⓓ Turn left for ferry terminal

Question 78

What does this sign mean?

Mark one answer

ⓐ T-junction
ⓑ No through road
ⓒ Telephone box ahead
ⓓ Toilet ahead

Question 79

Which sign means no through road?

Mark one answer

ⓐ ⓑ

ⓒ ⓓ

Question 80

Which of the following signs informs you that you are coming to a no through road?

Mark one answer

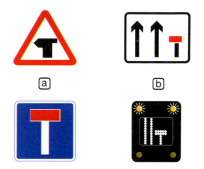

ⓐ

ⓑ

ⓒ

ⓓ

Question 81

What does this sign mean?

Mark one answer

ⓐ Direction to park and ride car park
ⓑ No parking for buses or coaches
ⓒ Directions to bus and coach park
ⓓ Parking area for cars and coaches

Question 82

You are going through a tunnel and you see this sign. What does it mean?

Mark one answer

ⓐ Direction to emergency pedestrian exit
ⓑ Beware of pedestrians, no footpath ahead
ⓒ No access for pedestrians
ⓓ Beware of pedestrians crossing ahead

Question 83

Which is the sign for a ring road?

Mark one answer

ⓐ

ⓑ

ⓒ

ⓓ

Question 84

What does this sign mean?

Mark one answer

- a Route for lorries
- b Ring road
- c Rest area
- d Roundabout

Question 85

What does this sign mean?

H R

Mark one answer

- a Hilly road
- b Humps in road
- c Holiday route
- d Hospital route

Question 86

What does this sign mean?

Mark one answer

- a The right-hand lane ahead is narrow
- b Right-hand lane for buses only
- c Right-hand lane for turning right
- d The right-hand lane is closed

Question 87

What does this sign mean?

Mark one answer

- a Change to the left lane
- b Leave at the next exit
- c Contraflow system
- d One-way street

Question 88

To avoid an accident when entering a contraflow system, you should

Mark three answers

- a reduce speed in good time
- b switch lanes anytime to make progress
- c choose an appropriate lane early
- d keep the correct separation distance
- e increase speed to pass through quickly
- f follow other motorists closely to avoid long queues

Question 89

What does this sign mean?

Mark one answer

ⓐ Leave motorway at next exit
ⓑ Lane for heavy and slow vehicles
ⓒ All lorries use the hard shoulder
ⓓ Rest area for lorries

Question 90

You see this traffic light ahead. Which light(s) will come on next?

Mark one answer

ⓐ Red alone
ⓑ Red and amber together
ⓒ Green and amber together
ⓓ Green alone

Question 91

You are approaching a red traffic light. The signal will change from red to

Mark one answer

ⓐ red and amber, then green
ⓑ green, then amber
ⓒ amber, then green
ⓓ green and amber, then green

Question 92

A red traffic light means

Mark one answer

ⓐ you should stop unless turning left
ⓑ stop, if you are able to brake safely
ⓒ you must stop and wait behind the stop line
ⓓ proceed with caution

Question 93

At traffic lights, amber on its own means

Mark one answer

- ⓐ prepare to go
- ⓑ go if the way is clear
- ⓒ go if no pedestrians are crossing
- ⓓ stop at the stop line

Question 94

A red traffic light means

Mark one answer

- ⓐ you must stop behind the white stop line
- ⓑ you may drive straight on if there is no other traffic
- ⓒ you may turn left if it is safe to do so
- ⓓ you must slow down and prepare to stop if traffic has started to cross

Question 95

You are approaching traffic lights. Red and amber are showing. This means

Mark one answer

- ⓐ pass the lights if the road is clear
- ⓑ there is a fault with the lights – take care
- ⓒ wait for the green light before you pass the lights
- ⓓ the lights are about to change to red

Question 96

You are at a junction controlled by traffic lights. When should you NOT proceed at green?

Mark one answer

- ⓐ When pedestrians are waiting to cross
- ⓑ When your exit from the junction is blocked
- ⓒ When you think the lights may be about to change
- ⓓ When you intend to turn right

Question 97

You are in the left-hand lane at traffic lights. You are waiting to turn left. At which of these traffic lights must you NOT move on?

Mark one answer

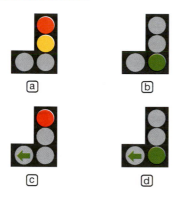

Question 98

What does this sign mean?

Mark one answer

- a) Traffic lights out of order
- b) Amber signal out of order
- c) Temporary traffic lights ahead
- d) New traffic lights ahead

Question 99

You see this sign at a crossroads. You should

Mark one answer

- a) maintain the same speed
- b) carry on with great care
- c) find another route
- d) telephone the police

Question 100

When traffic lights are out of order, who has priority?

Mark one answer

- a) Traffic going straight on
- b) Traffic turning right
- c) Nobody
- d) Traffic turning left

Question 101

These flashing red lights mean STOP. In which THREE of the following places could you find them?

Mark three answers

- a) Pelican crossings
- b) Lifting bridges
- c) Zebra crossings
- d) Level crossings
- e) Motorway exits
- f) Fire stations

Question 102

What do these zigzag lines at pedestrian crossings mean?

Mark one answer

- ⓐ No parking at any time
- ⓑ Parking allowed only for a short time
- ⓒ Slow down to 20 mph
- ⓓ Sounding horns is not allowed

Question 103

You are approaching a zebra crossing where pedestrians are waiting. Which arm signal might you give?

Mark one answer

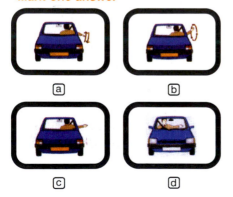

Question 104

The white line along the side of the road

Mark one answer

- ⓐ shows the edge of the carriageway
- ⓑ shows the approach to a hazard
- ⓒ means no parking
- ⓓ means no overtaking

Question 105

The white line painted in the centre of the road means

Mark one answer

- ⓐ the area is hazardous and you must not overtake
- ⓑ you should give priority to oncoming vehicles
- ⓒ do not cross the line unless the road ahead is clear
- ⓓ the area is a national speed limit zone

Question 106

When may you cross a double solid white line in the middle of the road?

Mark one answer

- ⓐ To pass traffic that is queuing back at a junction
- ⓑ To pass a car signalling to turn left ahead
- ⓒ To pass a road maintenance vehicle travelling at 10 mph or less
- ⓓ To pass a vehicle that is towing a trailer

Question 107

A white line like this along the centre of the road is a

Mark one answer

- ⓐ bus-lane marking
- ⓑ hazard warning
- ⓒ 'give way' marking
- ⓓ lane marking

Question 108

You see this white arrow on the road ahead. It means

Mark one answer

- ⓐ entrance on the left
- ⓑ all vehicles turn left
- ⓒ keep left of the hatched markings
- ⓓ road bending to the left

Question 109

What does this road marking mean?

Mark one answer

- ⓐ Do not cross the line
- ⓑ No stopping allowed
- ⓒ You are approaching a hazard
- ⓓ No overtaking allowed

Question 110

This marking appears on the road just before a

Mark one answer

a) no entry sign
b) give way sign
c) stop sign
d) no through road sign

Question 111

Where would you see this road marking?

Mark one answer

a) At traffic lights
b) On road humps
c) Near a level crossing
d) At a box junction

Question 112

Which is a hazard warning line?

Mark one answer

a)

b)

c)

d)

Question 113

At this junction there is a stop sign with a solid white line on the road surface. Why is there a stop sign here?

Mark one answer

a) Speed on the major road is de-restricted
b) It is a busy junction
c) Visibility along the major road is restricted
d) There are hazard warning lines in the centre of the road

Question 114

You see this line across the road at the entrance to a roundabout. What does it mean?

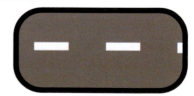

Mark one answer

a) Give way to traffic from the right
b) Traffic from the left has right of way
c) You have right of way
d) Stop at the line

Question 115

Where would you find this road marking?

Mark one answer

- ⓐ At a railway crossing
- ⓑ At a junction
- ⓒ On a motorway
- ⓓ On a pedestrian crossing

Question 116

How will a police officer in a patrol vehicle normally get you to stop?

Mark one answer

- ⓐ Flash the headlights, indicate left and point to the left
- ⓑ Wait until you stop, then approach you
- ⓒ Use the siren, overtake, cut in front and stop
- ⓓ Pull alongside you, use the siren and wave you to stop

Question 117

There is a police car following you. The police officer flashes the headlights and points to the left. What should you do?

Mark one answer

- ⓐ Turn at the next left
- ⓑ Pull up on the left
- ⓒ Stop immediately
- ⓓ Move over to the left

Question 118

You approach a junction. The traffic lights are not working. A police officer gives this signal. You should

Mark one answer

- ⓐ turn left only
- ⓑ turn right only
- ⓒ stop level with the officer's arm
- ⓓ stop at the stop line

Question 119

The driver of the car in front is giving this arm signal. What does it mean?

Mark one answer

- ⓐ The driver is slowing down
- ⓑ The driver intends to turn right
- ⓒ The driver wishes to overtake
- ⓓ The driver intends to turn left

Question 120

The driver of this car is giving an arm signal. What is he about to do?

Mark one answer

ⓐ Turn to the right
ⓑ Turn to the left
ⓒ Go straight ahead
ⓓ Let pedestrians cross

Question 121

Which arm signal tells a following vehicle that you intend to turn left?

Mark one answer

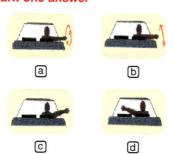

ⓐ　　　　　ⓑ

ⓒ　　　　　ⓓ

Question 122

How should you give an arm signal to turn left?

Mark one answer

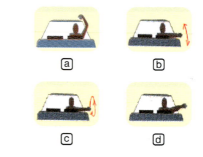

ⓐ　　　　　ⓑ

ⓒ　　　　　ⓓ

Question 123

You are signalling to turn right in busy traffic. How would you confirm your intention safely?

Mark one answer

ⓐ Sound the horn
ⓑ Give an arm signal
ⓒ Flash your headlights
ⓓ Position over the centre line

Question 124

How should you give an arm signal to turn left?

Mark one answer

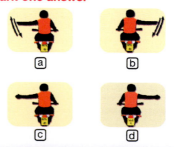

ⓐ　　　　　ⓑ

ⓒ　　　　　ⓓ

Question 125

Your indicators are difficult to see due to bright sunshine. When using them you should

Mark one answer

ⓐ also give an arm signal
ⓑ sound your horn
ⓒ flash your headlamp
ⓓ keep both hands on the handlebars

Question 126

You are giving an arm signal ready to turn left. Why should you NOT continue with the arm signal while you turn?

Mark one answer

ⓐ Because you might hit a pedestrian on the corner
ⓑ Because you will have less steering control
ⓒ Because you will need to keep the clutch applied
ⓓ Because other motorists will think that you are stopping on the corner

Question 127

You want to turn right at a junction but you think that your indicators cannot be seen clearly. What should you do?

Mark one answer

ⓐ Get out and check if your indicators can be seen
ⓑ Stay in the left-hand lane
ⓒ Keep well over to the right
ⓓ Give an arm signal as well as an indicator signal

Question 128

When may you sound the horn on your vehicle?

Mark one answer

ⓐ To give you right of way
ⓑ To attract a friend's attention
ⓒ To warn others of your presence
ⓓ To make slower drivers move over

Question 129

You must not use your horn when your vehicle is stationary

Mark one answer

ⓐ unless a moving vehicle may cause you danger
ⓑ at any time whatsoever
ⓒ unless it is used only briefly
ⓓ except for signalling that you have just arrived

Question 130

When motorists flash their headlights at you it means

Mark one answer

a that there is a radar speed trap ahead

b that they are giving way to you

c that they are warning you of their presence

d that there is something wrong with your vehicle

Question 131

Why should you make sure that you have cancelled your indicators after turning?

Mark one answer

a To avoid flattening the battery

b To avoid misleading other road users

c To avoid dazzling other road users

d To avoid damage to the indicator relay

Question 132

You are waiting at a T-junction. A vehicle is coming from the right with the left signal flashing. What should you do?

Mark one answer

a Move out and accelerate hard

b Wait until the vehicle starts to turn in

c Pull out before the vehicle reaches the junction

d Move out slowly

Question 133

When may you use hazard warning lights when driving?

Mark one answer

a Instead of sounding the horn in a built-up area between 11.30 pm and 7 am

b On a motorway or unrestricted dual carriageway, to warn of a hazard ahead

c On rural routes, after a warning sign of animals

d On the approach to toucan crossings where cyclists are waiting to cross

Question 134

Where would you see these road markings?

Mark one answer

a At a level crossing

b On a motorway slip road

c At a pedestrian crossing

d On a single-track road

Question 135

When may you NOT overtake on the left?

Mark one answer

ⓐ On a free-flowing motorway or dual carriageway

ⓑ When the traffic is moving slowly in queues

ⓒ On a one-way street

ⓓ When the car in front is signalling to turn right

Question 136

You are driving on a motorway. There is a slow-moving vehicle ahead. On the back you see this sign. You should

Mark one answer

ⓐ pass on the right

ⓑ pass on the left

ⓒ leave at the next exit

ⓓ drive no further

Question 137

What does this motorway sign mean?

Mark one answer

ⓐ Change to the lane on your left

ⓑ Leave the motorway at the next exit

ⓒ Change to the opposite carriageway

ⓓ Pull up on the hard shoulder

Question 138

What does this motorway sign mean?

Mark one answer

ⓐ Temporary minimum speed 50 mph

ⓑ No services for 50 miles

ⓒ Obstruction 50 metres (164 feet) ahead

ⓓ Temporary maximum speed 50 mph

Question 139

What does this sign mean?

Mark one answer

ⓐ Through traffic to use left lane

ⓑ Right-hand lane T-junction only

ⓒ Right-hand lane closed ahead

ⓓ 11 tonne weight limit

Question 140

On a motorway this sign means

Mark one answer

- a move over onto the hard shoulder
- b overtaking on the left only
- c leave the motorway at the next exit
- d move to the lane on your left

Question 141

What does '25' mean on this motorway sign?

Mark one answer

- a The distance to the nearest town
- b The route number of the road
- c The number of the next junction
- d The speed limit on the slip road

Question 142

You are on a motorway. Red flashing lights appear above your lane only. What should you do?

Mark one answer

- a Continue in that lane and await further information
- b Go no further in that lane
- c Pull onto the hard shoulder
- d Stop and wait for an instruction to proceed

Question 143

The right-hand lane of a three-lane motorway is

Mark one answer

- a for lorries only
- b an overtaking lane
- c the right-turn lane
- d an acceleration lane

Question 144

Where can you find reflective amber studs on a motorway?

Mark one answer

- a Separating the slip road from the motorway
- b On the left-hand edge of the road
- c On the right-hand edge of the road
- d Separating the lanes

Question 145

Where on a motorway would you find green reflective studs?

Mark one answer

- ⓐ Separating driving lanes
- ⓑ Between the hard shoulder and the carriageway
- ⓒ At slip-road entrances and exits
- ⓓ Between the carriageway and the central reservation

Question 146

You are travelling along a motorway. You see this sign. You should

Mark one answer

- ⓐ leave the motorway at the next exit
- ⓑ turn left immediately
- ⓒ change lane
- ⓓ move onto the hard shoulder

Question 147

You see these signs overhead on the motorway. They mean

Mark one answer

- ⓐ leave the motorway at the next exit
- ⓑ all vehicles use the hard shoulder
- ⓒ sharp bend to the left ahead
- ⓓ stop, all lanes ahead closed

Question 148

What does this sign mean?

Mark one answer

- ⓐ No motor vehicles
- ⓑ End of motorway
- ⓒ No through road
- ⓓ End of bus lane

Question 149

Which of these signs means that the national speed limit applies?

Mark one answer

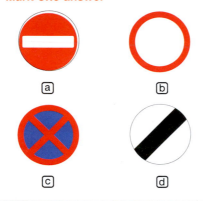

ⓐ

ⓑ

ⓒ

ⓓ

Question 150

What is the maximum speed on a single carriageway road?

Mark one answer

ⓐ 50 mph

ⓑ 60 mph

ⓒ 40 mph

ⓓ 70 mph

Question 151

What does this sign mean?

Mark one answer

ⓐ Motorcycles only

ⓑ No cars

ⓒ Cars only

ⓓ No motorcycles

Question 152

You are on a motorway. You see this sign on a lorry that has stopped in the right-hand lane. You should

Mark one answer

ⓐ move into the right-hand lane

ⓑ stop behind the flashing lights

ⓒ pass the lorry on the left

ⓓ leave the motorway at the next exit

Question 153

This sign is of particular importance to motorcyclists. It means

Mark one answer

ⓐ side winds

ⓑ airport

ⓒ slippery road

ⓓ service area

Question 154

What does this sign mean?

Mark one answer

ⓐ End of motorway

ⓑ End of restriction

ⓒ Lane ends ahead

ⓓ Free recovery ends

Question 155

This sign is advising you to

Mark one answer

- a follow the route diversion
- b follow the signs to the picnic area
- c give way to pedestrians
- d give way to cyclists

Question 156

Why would this temporary speed limit sign be shown?

Mark one answer

- a To warn of the end of the motorway
- b To warn you of a low bridge
- c To warn you of a junction ahead
- d To warn of roadworks ahead

Question 157

Which one of these signs are you allowed to ride past on a solo motorcycle?

Mark one answer

a

b

c

d

Question 158

Which of these signals should you give when slowing or stopping your motorcycle?

Mark one answer

a

b

c

d

Answers and explanations

Q001	d
Q002	d
Q003	a Red circles tell you what you must not do. Rectangles usually give you information.
Q004	a
Q005	b This sign means no vehicles except bicycles being pushed by hand.
Q006	a
Q007	d
Q008	a
Q009	b
Q010	d
Q011	d
Q012	d
Q013	a
Q014	c
Q015	b
Q016	d
Q017	c
Q018	b
Q019	a There will also be a plate indicating when the restriction applies.
Q020	b
Q021	b
Q022	b
Q023	c
Q024	c This is a clearway sign and you must not stop at all.

Q025	a
Q026	c
Q027	b
Q028	c
Q029	c
Q030	b You must always stop at a stop sign.
Q031	d
Q032	d
Q033	c
Q034	d
Q035	c
Q036	b
Q037	a
Q038	c
Q039	d
Q040	a
Q041	d Circular signs with blue backgrounds tell you what you must do.
Q042	b
Q043	d
Q044	b
Q045	a
Q046	a
Q047	a
Q048	a
Q049	b
Q050	b
Q051	a
Q052	d

Q053	a,c,e,f	
Q054	c	
Q055	a	
Q056	a	
Q057	c	
Q058	d	
Q059	b	
Q060	c	
Q061	b	
Q062	b	Red triangles usually give a warning.
Q063	b	
Q064	b	
Q065	d	
Q066	a	
Q067	c	
Q068	a	
Q069	c	
Q070	d	The sign is warning of a possible danger ahead so it would be dangerous to overtake.
Q071	a	
Q072	c	
Q073	b	
Q074	a	
Q075	d	
Q076	a	
Q077	b	
Q078	b	
Q079	c	

Q080	c	
Q081	a	
Q082	a	
Q083	c	
Q084	b	
Q085	c	
Q086	d	
Q087	c	
Q088	a,c,d	
Q089	b	
Q090	a	
Q091	a	The sequence of traffic lights is red, then red and amber, then green, then amber alone, then red.
Q092	c	You must always stop at a red traffic light.
Q093	d	An amber light means stop, and the lights will next change to red.
Q094	a	
Q095	c	The next light will be green and you must wait to drive on until it appears.
Q096	b	
Q097	a	
Q098	a	
Q099	b	
Q100	c	
Q101	b,d,f	
Q102	a	

Q103 a

Q104 a

Q105 c

Q106 c

Q107 b

Q108 c

Q109 c

Q110 b

Q111 b

Q112 a Long lines with short gaps between them in the middle of the road are hazard warning lines. The more paint the more danger.

Q113 c Because the major road is on a bend, your vision is restricted to both left and right.

Q114 a

Q115 b

Q116 a

Q117 b You must stop, but 'c' is wrong because it may not be safe to stop immediately.

Q118 d

Q119 d

Q120 b

Q121 a

Q122 c

Q123 b

Q124 c

Q125 a

Q126 b

Q127 d Then park in a safe place and check your indicators.

Q128 c Sounding your horn has the same meaning as flashing your headlights – to warn of your presence.

Q129 a

Q130 c 'c' is the correct answer because that is what flashing your headlights is supposed to mean. Not everyone knows or obeys the rules and may flash their headlights for other reasons, so always try to make sure of what they mean before you decide on any action.

Q131 b

Q132 b The approaching vehicle might have left the signal on by mistake, or intended to stop after the junction. Always wait long enough to be sure the vehicle is really turning left.

Answers and explanations

Q133 b Note that the question states 'when driving'. The types of roads in 'b' are the only places where it is legal to use hazard warning lights while your car is moving.

Q134 b

Q135 a You must not overtake on the left on a motorway or dual carriageway unless you are moving in queues of slow-moving traffic.

Q136 b

Q137 a Obviously you must make sure it is safe before doing so.

Q138 d

Q139 c Always look well ahead and you will have plenty of time to react.

Q140 d You must go no further in that lane. You may change lanes and proceed, unless flashing red lights appear above all of them.

Q141 c

Q142 b

Q143 b

Q144 c

Q145 c

Q146 a

Q147 a

Q148 b

Q149 d

Q150 b

Q151 d

Q152 c

Q153 a

Q154 b

Q155 a

Q156 d

Q157 d

Q158 a

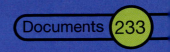

Driving Theory
Test
Questions

2000/2001

Documents

Question 1

To drive on the road learners MUST

Mark one answer

a have NO penalty points on their licence

b have taken professional instruction

c have a signed, valid provisional licence

d apply for a driving test within 12 months

Question 2

To supervise a learner driver you must

Mark two answers

a have held a full licence for at least 3 years

b be at least 21

c be an approved driving instructor

d hold an advanced driving certificate

Question 3

Your driving licence must be signed by

Mark one answer

a a police officer

b a driving instructor

c your next of kin

d yourself

Question 4

You have passed CBT (Compulsory Basic Training). You want a Direct Access test. You must

Mark four answers

a be aged 21 or over

b not exceed 60 mph

c have an approved instructor with you

d remain in radio contact while learning

e only learn in daylight hours

f wear fluorescent or reflective clothing

Question 5

You want a licence to ride a large motorcycle via direct access. You will

Mark one answer

a not require L plates if you have passed a car test

b require L plates only when learning on your own machine

c require L plates while learning with a qualified instructor

d not require L plates if you have passed a moped test

Question 6

You are a learner motorcyclist. The law states that you can carry a passenger when

Mark one answer

- [a] your motorcycle is no larger than 125cc
- [b] your pillion passenger is a full licence-holder
- [c] you have passed your test for a full licence
- [d] you have had three years' experience of riding

Question 7

What should you bring with you when taking your motorcycle test?

Mark three answers

- [a] A service record book
- [b] An insurance certificate
- [c] A signed driving licence
- [d] An MOT certificate
- [e] A CBT (Compulsory Basic Training) certificate
- [f] Signed photo identity

Question 8

Before taking a motorcycle test you need

Mark one answer

- [a] a full moped licence
- [b] a full car licence
- [c] a CBT (Compulsory Basic Training) certificate
- [d] 12 months' riding experience

Question 9

Compulsory Basic Training (CBT) can only be carried out by

Mark one answer

- [a] any ADI (Approved Driving Instructor)
- [b] any road safety officer
- [c] any DSA (Driving Standards Agency) approved training body
- [d] any motorcycle main dealer

Question 10

After passing your motorcycle test you must exchange the pass certificate for a full motorcycle licence within

Mark one answer

- [a] six months
- [b] one year
- [c] two years
- [d] five years

Question 11

For which TWO of these must you show your motor insurance certificate?

Mark two answers

ⓐ When you are taking your driving test
ⓑ When buying or selling a vehicle
ⓒ When a police officer asks you for it
ⓓ When you are taxing your vehicle
ⓔ When having an MOT inspection

Question 12

Vehicle excise duty is often called 'Road Tax' or 'The Tax Disc'. You must

Mark one answer

ⓐ keep it with your registration document
ⓑ display it clearly on your vehicle
ⓒ keep it concealed safely in your vehicle
ⓓ carry it on you at all times

Question 13

For which TWO of these must you show your motorcycle insurance certificate?

Mark two answers

ⓐ When you are taking your motorcycle test
ⓑ When buying or selling a machine
ⓒ When a police officer asks you for it
ⓓ When you are taxing your machine
ⓔ When having an MOT inspection

Question 14

A police officer asks to see your documents. You do not have them with you. You may produce them at a police station within

Mark one answer

ⓐ 5 days
ⓑ 7 days
ⓒ 14 days
ⓓ 21 days

Question 15

Before riding anyone else's motorcycle you should make sure that

Mark one answer

ⓐ the machine owner has third party insurance cover
ⓑ your own machine has insurance cover
ⓒ the machine is insured for your use
ⓓ the owner has the insurance documents with them

Question 16

Before driving anyone else's motor vehicle you should make sure that

Mark one answer

ⓐ the vehicle owner has third party insurance cover
ⓑ your own vehicle has insurance cover
ⓒ the vehicle is insured for your use
ⓓ the owner has left the insurance documents in the vehicle

Question 17

What is the legal minimum insurance cover you must have to drive or ride on public roads?

Mark one answer

a Third party, fire and theft

b Fully comprehensive

c Third party only

d Personal injury cover

Question 18

You have third party insurance. What does this cover?

Mark three answers

a Damage to your own vehicle

b Damage to your vehicle by fire

c Injury to another person

d Damage to someone's property

e Damage to other vehicles

f Injury to yourself

Question 19

The cost of your insurance may be reduced if

Mark one answer

a your car is large and powerful

b you are using the car for work purposes

c you have penalty points on your licence

d you are over 25 years old

Question 20

Motor cars and motorcycles must FIRST have an MOT test certificate when they are

Mark one answer

a one year old

b three years old

c five years old

d seven years old

Question 21

An MOT certificate is normally valid for

Mark one answer

a three years after the date it was issued

b 10,000 miles

c one year after the date it was issued

d 30,000 miles

Question 22

Your car needs an MOT certificate. If you drive without one this could invalidate your

Mark one answer

a vehicle service record

b insurance

c road tax disc

d vehicle registration document

Question 23

When is it legal to drive a car over three years old without an MOT certificate?

Mark one answer

ⓐ Up to seven days after the old certificate has run out

ⓑ When driving to an MOT centre to arrange an appointment

ⓒ Just after buying a secondhand car with no MOT

ⓓ When driving to an appointment at an MOT centre

Question 24

Your vehicle needs a current MOT certificate. You do not have one. Until you do have one you will not be able to renew your

Mark one answer

ⓐ driving licence

ⓑ vehicle insurance

ⓒ road tax disc

ⓓ vehicle registration document

Question 25

Which TWO of these are NOT required to have an MOT certificate?

Mark two answers

ⓐ Motorcycle

ⓑ Small trailer

ⓒ Ambulance

ⓓ Caravan

Question 26

Which THREE of the following do you need before you can drive or ride legally?

Mark three answers

ⓐ A valid signed driving licence

ⓑ A valid tax disc displayed on your vehicle

ⓒ Proof of your identity

ⓓ Proper insurance cover

ⓔ Breakdown cover

ⓕ A vehicle handbook

Question 27

CBT (Compulsory Basic Training) completion certificates (DL196) issued on or after 01 July 1996 are valid for

Mark one answer

ⓐ two years

ⓑ three years

ⓒ five years

ⓓ indefinitely

Question 28

When you buy a motorcycle you will need a vehicle registration document from

Mark one answer

ⓐ any MOT testing station

ⓑ the person selling the motorcycle

ⓒ your local council offices

ⓓ your local trading standards officer

Question 29

Which THREE pieces of information are found on a vehicle registration document?

Mark three answers

- ⓐ Registered keeper
- ⓑ Make of the vehicle
- ⓒ Service history details
- ⓓ Date of the MOT
- ⓔ Type of insurance cover
- ⓕ Engine size

Question 30

You have a duty to contact the licensing authority when

Mark three answers

- ⓐ you go abroad on holiday
- ⓑ you change your vehicle
- ⓒ you change your name
- ⓓ your job status is changed
- ⓔ your permanent address changes
- ⓕ your job involves travelling abroad

Question 31

You must notify the licensing authority when

Mark three answers

- ⓐ your health affects your driving
- ⓑ your eyesight does not meet a set standard
- ⓒ you intend lending your vehicle
- ⓓ your vehicle requires an MOT certificate
- ⓔ you change your vehicle

Question 32

You have just bought a secondhand vehicle. When should you tell the licensing authority of change of ownership?

Mark one answer

- ⓐ Immediately
- ⓑ After 28 days
- ⓒ When an MOT is due
- ⓓ Only when you insure it

Question 33

Your vehicle is insured third party only. This covers

Mark two answers

- ⓐ damage to your vehicle
- ⓑ damage to other vehicles
- ⓒ injury to yourself
- ⓓ injury to others
- ⓔ all damage and injury

Question 34

You hold a provisional motorcycle licence. This means you must NOT

Mark three answers

- ⓐ exceed 30 mph
- ⓑ ride on a motorway
- ⓒ ride after dark
- ⓓ carry a pillion passenger
- ⓔ ride without L plates displayed

Question 35

Which of the following information is found on your motorcycle registration document?

Mark three answers

a) Make and model
b) Service history record
c) Ignition key security number
d) Engine size and number
e) Purchase price
f) Year of first registration

Question 36

A theory test pass certificate will not be valid after

Mark one answer

a) 6 months
b) 1 year
c) 18 months
d) 2 years

Question 37

A theory test pass certificate is valid for

Mark one answer

a) 2 years
b) 3 years
c) 4 years
d) 5 years

Question 38

Your motor insurance policy has an excess of £100. What does this mean?

Mark one answer

a) The insurance company will pay the first £100 of any claim
b) You will be paid £100 if you do not have an accident
c) Your vehicle is insured for a value of £100 if it is stolen
d) You will have to pay the first £100 of any claim

Question 39

You have just passed your driving test. Within two years you get six penalty points on your licence. You will have to

Mark two answers

a) retake only your theory test
b) retake your theory and practical tests
c) retake only your practical test
d) re-apply for your full licence immediately
e) re-apply for your provisional licence

Question 40

A cover note is a document issued before you receive your

Mark one answer

a) driving licence
b) insurance certificate
c) registration document
d) MOT certificate

Question 41

When you apply to renew your vehicle excise licence (tax disc) you must produce

Mark one answer

ⓐ a valid insurance certificate

ⓑ the old tax disc

ⓒ the vehicle handbook

ⓓ a valid driving licence

Question 42

What is the legal minimum insurance cover you must have to drive on public roads?

Mark one answer

ⓐ Fire and theft

ⓑ Theft only

ⓒ Third party

ⓓ Fire only

Question 43

A full category A1 licence will allow you to ride a motorcycle up to

Mark one answer

ⓐ 125cc

ⓑ 250cc

ⓒ 350cc

ⓓ 425cc

Question 44

The cost of your insurance may be reduced if you

Mark two answers

ⓐ are over 25 years old

ⓑ are under 25 years old

ⓒ do not wear glasses

ⓓ pass the driving test first time

ⓔ complete the Pass Plus scheme

Question 45

How old must you be to supervise a learner driver?

Mark one answer

ⓐ 18 years old

ⓑ 19 years old

ⓒ 20 years old

ⓓ 21 years old

Question 46

A newly qualified driver must

Mark one answer

ⓐ display green L plates

ⓑ not exceed 40 mph for 12 months

ⓒ be accompanied on a motorway

ⓓ have valid motor insurance

Answers and explanations

Q001   c You are not allowed to drive until you have applied for and received your provisional licence and have signed it in ink.

Q002   a,b

Q003   d Your driving licence is not valid until you have signed it in ink.

Q004   a,c,d,f

Q005   c

Q006   c

Q007   c,e,f

Q008   c

Q009   c

Q010   c

Q011   c,d

Q012   b

Q013   c,d

Q014   b You may select the police station of your choice.

Q015   c Your own motorbike insurance is very unlikely to cover you to drive another person's motorbike.

Q016   c Your own vehicle insurance may cover you as a passenger in another person's vehicle but very rarely covers you to drive it.

Q017   c This only covers damage to other people and their property.

Q018   c,d,e

Q019   d Drivers over 25 years old have less accidents than younger drivers. As they make fewer insurance claims, the cost of their premiums is usually less.

Q020   b

Q021   c

Q022   b

Q023   d If your car is over three years old and has no valid MOT certificate, you must pre-book an appointment at an MOT centre before you drive it there.

Q024   c When you renew your road tax disc you must produce a valid certificate of insurance and also a current MOT certificate if your car is over three years old.

Q025   b,d

Q026   a,b,d

Q027   b

Q028   b

Answers and explanations

Q029 a,b,f

Q030 b,c,e

Q031 a,b,e

Q032 a

Q033 b,d

Q034 b,d,e

Q035 a,d,f

Q036 d

Q037 a

Q038 d Agreeing to pay an excess may enable you to obtain a lower premium.

Q039 b,e

Q040 b

Q041 a

Q042 c

Q043 a

Q044 a,e

Q045 d

Q046 d

Driving Theory
Test
Questions
2000/2001

Accidents

BSM
We won't fail you

Question 1

Which of these items should you carry in your vehicle for use in the event of an accident?

Mark three answers

- a. Road map
- b. Can of petrol
- c. Jump leads
- d. Fire extinguisher
- e. First Aid kit
- f. Warning triangle

Question 2

At the scene of an accident you should

Mark one answer

- a. not put yourself at risk
- b. go to those casualties who are screaming
- c. pull everybody out of their vehicles
- d. leave vehicle engines switched on

Question 3

You are the first to arrive at the scene of an accident. Which FOUR of these should you do?

Mark four answers

- a. Leave as soon as another motorist arrives
- b. Switch off the vehicle engine(s)
- c. Move uninjured people away from the vehicle(s)
- d. Call the emergency services
- e. Warn other traffic

Question 4

An accident has just happened. An injured person is lying in the busy road. What is the FIRST thing you should do to help?

Mark one answer

- a. Treat the person for shock
- b. Warn other traffic
- c. Place them in the recovery position
- d. Make sure the injured person is kept warm

Question 5

You are the first person to arrive at an accident where people are badly injured. Which THREE should you do?

Mark three answers

- a. Switch on your own hazard warning lights
- b. Make sure that someone telephones for an ambulance
- c. Try and get people who are injured to drink something
- d. Move the people who are injured clear of their vehicles
- e. Get people who are not injured clear of the scene

Question 6

You arrive at the scene of a motorcycle accident. The rider is injured. When should the helmet be removed?

Mark one answer

a) Only when it is essential
b) Always straight away
c) Only when the motorcyclist asks
d) Always, unless they are in shock

Question 7

You arrive at a serious motorcycle accident. The motorcyclist is unconscious and bleeding. Your main priorities should be to

Mark three answers

a) try to stop the bleeding
b) make a list of witnesses
c) check the casualty's breathing
d) take the numbers of the vehicles involved
e) sweep up any loose debris
f) check the casualty's airways

Question 8

You arrive at an accident. A motorcyclist is unconscious. Your FIRST priority is the casualty's

Mark one answer

a) breathing
b) bleeding
c) broken bones
d) bruising

Question 9

At an accident a casualty is unconscious. Which THREE of the following should you check urgently?

Mark three answers

a) Circulation
b) Airway
c) Shock
d) Breathing
e) Broken bones

Question 10

You arrive at the scene of an accident. It has just happened and someone is unconscious. Which of the following should be given urgent priority to help them?

Mark three answers

a) Clear the airway and keep it open
b) Try to get them to drink water
c) Check that they are breathing
d) Look for any witnesses
e) Stop any heavy bleeding
f) Take the numbers of vehicles involved

Question 11

At an accident someone is unconscious. Your main priorities should be to

Mark three answers

ⓐ sweep up the broken glass

ⓑ take the names of witnesses

ⓒ count the number of vehicles involved

ⓓ check the airway is clear

ⓔ make sure they are breathing

ⓕ stop any heavy bleeding

Question 12

You have stopped at the scene of an accident to give help. Which THREE things should you do?

Mark three answers

ⓐ Keep injured people warm and comfortable

ⓑ Keep injured people calm by talking to them reassuringly

ⓒ Keep injured people on the move by walking them around

ⓓ Give injured people a warm drink

ⓔ Make sure that injured people are not left alone

Question 13

You arrive at the scene of an accident. It has just happened and someone is injured. Which THREE of the following should be given urgent priority?

Mark three answers

ⓐ Stop any severe bleeding

ⓑ Get them a warm drink

ⓒ Check that their breathing is OK

ⓓ Take numbers of vehicles involved

ⓔ Look for witnesses

ⓕ Clear their airway and keep it open

Question 14

At an accident a casualty has stopped breathing. You should

Mark two answers

ⓐ remove anything that is blocking the mouth

ⓑ keep the head tilted forwards as far as possible

ⓒ raise the legs to help with circulation

ⓓ try to give the casualty something to drink

ⓔ keep the head tilted back as far as possible

Question 15

You are at the scene of an accident.
Someone is suffering from shock.
You should

Mark four answers
- a) reassure them constantly
- b) offer them a cigarette
- c) keep them warm
- d) avoid moving them if possible
- e) loosen any tight clothing
- f) give them a warm drink

Question 16

Which of the following should you NOT
do at the scene of an accident?

Mark one answer
- a) Warn other traffic by switching on your hazard warning lights
- b) Call the emergency services immediately
- c) Offer someone a cigarette to calm them down
- d) Ask drivers to switch off their engines

Question 17

There has been an accident. The driver is
suffering from shock. You should

Mark two answers
- a) give them a drink
- b) reassure them
- c) not leave them alone
- d) offer them a cigarette
- e) ask who caused the accident

Question 18

You are at the scene of an accident.
Someone is suffering from shock.
You should

Mark three answers
- a) offer them a cigarette
- b) offer them a warm drink
- c) keep them warm
- d) loosen any tight clothing
- e) reassure them constantly

Question 19

You have to treat someone for shock at
the scene of an accident. You should

Mark one answer
- a) reassure them constantly
- b) walk them around to calm them down
- c) give them something cold to drink
- d) cool them down as soon as possible

Question 20

You arrive at the scene of a motorcycle
accident. No other vehicle is involved.
The rider is unconscious, lying in the
middle of the road. The first thing you
should do is

Mark one answer
- a) move the rider out of the road
- b) warn other traffic
- c) clear the road of debris
- d) give the rider reassurance

Question 21

At an accident a small child is not breathing. When giving mouth to mouth you should breathe

Mark one answer

- ⓐ sharply
- ⓑ gently
- ⓒ heavily
- ⓓ rapidly

Question 22

To start mouth to mouth on a casualty you should

Mark three answers

- ⓐ tilt their head forward
- ⓑ clear the airway
- ⓒ turn them on their side
- ⓓ tilt their head back
- ⓔ pinch the nostrils together
- ⓕ put their arms across their chest

Question 23

When you are giving mouth to mouth you should only stop when

Mark one answer

- ⓐ you think the casualty is dead
- ⓑ the casualty can breathe without help
- ⓒ the casualty has turned blue
- ⓓ you think the ambulance is coming

Question 24

You arrive at the scene of an accident. There has been an engine fire and someone's hands and arms have been burnt. You should NOT

Mark one answer

- ⓐ douse the burn thoroughly with cool liquid
- ⓑ lay the casualty down
- ⓒ remove anything sticking to the burn
- ⓓ reassure them constantly

Question 25

You arrive at an accident where someone is suffering from severe burns. You should

Mark one answer

- ⓐ apply lotions to the injury
- ⓑ burst any blisters
- ⓒ remove anything stuck to the burns
- ⓓ douse the burns with cool liquid

Question 26

You arrive at the scene of an accident. A pedestrian has a severe bleeding wound on their leg, although it is not broken. What should you do?

Mark two answers

- ⓐ Dab the wound to stop bleeding
- ⓑ Keep both legs flat on the ground
- ⓒ Apply firm pressure to the wound
- ⓓ Raise the leg to lessen bleeding
- ⓔ Fetch them a warm drink

Question 27

You arrive at the scene of an accident. A passenger is bleeding badly from an arm wound. What should you do?

Mark one answer

- ⓐ Apply pressure over the wound and keep the arm down
- ⓑ Dab the wound
- ⓒ Get them a drink
- ⓓ Apply pressure over the wound and raise the arm

Question 28

You arrive at the scene of an accident. A pedestrian is bleeding heavily from a leg wound but the leg is not broken. What should you do?

Mark one answer

- ⓐ Dab the wound to stop the bleeding
- ⓑ Keep both legs flat on the ground
- ⓒ Apply firm pressure to the wound
- ⓓ Fetch them a warm drink

Question 29

At an accident a casualty is unconscious but still breathing. You should only move them if

Mark one answer

- ⓐ an ambulance is on its way
- ⓑ bystanders advise you to
- ⓒ there is further danger
- ⓓ bystanders will help you to

Question 30

At an accident you suspect a casualty has back injuries. The area is safe. You should

Mark one answer

- ⓐ offer them a drink
- ⓑ not move them
- ⓒ raise their legs
- ⓓ offer them a cigarette

Question 31

At an accident it is important to look after the casualty. When the area is safe, you should

Mark one answer

- ⓐ get them out of the vehicle
- ⓑ give them a drink
- ⓒ give them something to eat
- ⓓ keep them in the vehicle

Question 32

A tanker is involved in an accident. Which sign would show that the tanker is carrying dangerous goods?

Mark one answer

ⓐ ⓑ

ⓒ ⓓ

Question 33

While driving, a warning light on your vehicle's instrument panel comes on. You should

Mark one answer

- ⓐ continue if the engine sounds alright
- ⓑ hope that it is just a temporary electrical fault
- ⓒ deal with the problem when there is more time
- ⓓ check out the problem quickly and safely

Question 34

For which TWO should you use hazard warning lights?

Mark two answers

- ⓐ When you slow down quickly on a motorway because of a hazard ahead
- ⓑ When you have broken down
- ⓒ When you wish to stop on double yellow lines
- ⓓ When you need to park on the pavement

Question 35

For which THREE should you use your hazard warning lights?

Mark three answers

- ⓐ When you are parking in a restricted area
- ⓑ When you are temporarily obstructing traffic
- ⓒ To warn following traffic of a hazard ahead
- ⓓ When you have broken down
- ⓔ When only stopping for a short time

Question 36

When are you allowed to use hazard warning lights?

Mark one answer

- ⓐ When stopped and temporarily obstructing traffic
- ⓑ When travelling during darkness without headlights
- ⓒ When parked for shopping on double yellow lines
- ⓓ When travelling slowly because you are lost

Question 37

You have broken down on a two-way road. You have a warning triangle. You should place the warning triangle at least how far from your vehicle?

Mark one answer

ⓐ 5 metres (16 feet)
ⓑ 25 metres (82 feet)
ⓒ 45 metres (147 feet)
ⓓ 100 metres (328 feet)

Question 38

You are in an accident on a two-way road. You have a warning triangle with you. At what distance before the obstruction should you place the warning triangle?

Mark one answer

ⓐ 25 metres (82 feet)
ⓑ 45 metres (147 feet)
ⓒ 100 metres (328 feet)
ⓓ 150 metres (492 feet)

Question 39

Your motorcycle has broken down on a motorway. How will you know the direction of the nearest emergency telephone?

Mark one answer

ⓐ By walking with the flow of traffic
ⓑ By following an arrow on a marker post
ⓒ By walking against the flow of traffic
ⓓ By remembering where the last phone was

Question 40

You have broken down on a two-way road. You have a warning triangle. It should be displayed

Mark one answer

ⓐ on the roof of your vehicle
ⓑ at least 150 metres (492 feet) behind your vehicle
ⓒ at least 45 metres (147 feet) behind your vehicle
ⓓ just behind your vehicle

Question 41

The police may ask you to produce which three of these documents following an accident?

Mark three answers

a) Vehicle registration document
b) Driving licence
c) Theory test certificate
d) Insurance certificate
e) MOT test certificate
f) Road tax disc

Question 42

You are involved in an accident with another driver. Someone is injured. Your vehicle is damaged. Which FOUR of the following should you find out?

Mark four answers

a) Whether the driver owns the other vehicle involved
b) The other driver's name, address and telephone number
c) The car make and registration number of the other vehicle
d) The occupation of the other driver
e) The details of the other driver's vehicle insurance
f) Whether the other driver is licensed to drive

Question 43

At a railway level crossing the red light signal continues to flash after a train has gone by. What should you do?

Mark one answer

a) Phone the signal operator
b) Alert drivers behind you
c) Wait
d) Proceed with caution

Question 44

You break down on a level crossing. The lights have not yet begun to flash. Which THREE things should you do?

Mark three answers

a) Telephone the signal operator
b) Leave your vehicle and get everyone clear
c) Walk down the track and signal the next train
d) Move the vehicle if a signal operator tells you to
e) Tell drivers behind what has happened

Question 45

You have stalled in the middle of a level crossing and cannot restart the engine. The warning bell starts to ring.
You should

Mark one answer

ⓐ get out and clear of the crossing

ⓑ run down the track to warn the signal operator

ⓒ carry on trying to restart the engine

ⓓ push the vehicle clear of the crossing

Question 46

Your vehicle has broken down on an automatic railway level crossing. What should you do FIRST?

Mark one answer

ⓐ Get everyone out of the vehicle and clear of the crossing

ⓑ Phone the signal operator so that trains can be stopped

ⓒ Walk along the track to give warning to any approaching trains

ⓓ Try to push the vehicle clear of the crossing as soon as possible

Question 47

Your tyre bursts while you are driving. Which TWO things should you do?

Mark two answers

ⓐ Pull on the handbrake

ⓑ Brake as quickly as possible

ⓒ Pull up slowly at the side of the road

ⓓ Hold the steering wheel firmly to keep control

ⓔ Continue on at a normal speed

Question 48

Which TWO things should you do when a front tyre bursts?

Mark two answers

ⓐ Apply the handbrake to stop the vehicle

ⓑ Brake firmly and quickly

ⓒ Let the vehicle roll to a stop

ⓓ Hold the steering wheel lightly

ⓔ Grip the steering wheel firmly

Question 49

Your vehicle has a puncture on a motorway. What should you do?

Mark one answer

(a) Drive slowly to the next service area to get assistance

(b) Pull up on the hard shoulder. Change the wheel as quickly as possible

(c) Pull up on the hard shoulder. Use the emergency phone to get assistance

(d) Switch on your hazard lights. Stop in your lane

Question 50

You should use the engine cut-out switch to

Mark one answer

(a) stop the engine in an emergency

(b) stop the engine on short journeys

(c) save wear on the ignition switch

(d) start the engine if you lose the key

Question 51

You see a car on the hard shoulder of a motorway with a HELP pennant displayed. This means the driver is most likely to be

Mark one answer

(a) a disabled person

(b) first aid trained

(c) a foreign visitor

(d) a rescue patrol person

Question 52

On the motorway, the hard shoulder should be used

Mark one answer

(a) to answer a mobile phone

(b) when an emergency arises

(c) for a short rest when tired

(d) to check a road atlas

Question 53

What TWO safeguards could you take against fire risk to your vehicle?

Mark two answers

(a) Keep water levels above maximum

(b) Carry a fire extinguisher

(c) Avoid driving with a full tank of petrol

(d) Use unleaded petrol

(e) Check out any strong smell of petrol

(f) Use low octane fuel

Question 54

You have broken down on a motorway. When you use the emergency telephone you will be asked

Mark three answers

(a) for the number on the telephone that you are using

(b) for your driving licence details

(c) for the name of your vehicle insurance company

(d) for details of yourself and your vehicle

(e) whether you belong to a motoring organisation

Question 55

You are on the motorway. Luggage falls from your vehicle. What should you do?

Mark one answer

- a. Stop at the next emergency telephone and contact the police
- b. Stop on the motorway and put on hazard lights whilst you pick it up
- c. Walk back up the motorway to pick it up
- d. Pull up on the hard shoulder and wave traffic down

Question 56

You are travelling on a motorway. A bag falls from your motorcycle. There are valuables in the bag. What should you do?

Mark one answer

- a. Go back carefully and collect the bag as quickly as possible
- b. Stop wherever you are and pick up the bag, but only when there is a safe gap
- c. Stop on the hard shoulder and use the emergency telephone to inform the police
- d. Stop on the hard shoulder and then retrieve the bag yourself

Question 57

You are on a motorway. A large box falls onto the road from a lorry. The lorry does not stop. You should

Mark one answer

- a. go to the next emergency telephone and inform the police
- b. catch up with the lorry and try to get the driver's attention
- c. stop close to the box until the police arrive
- d. pull over to the hard shoulder, then remove the box

Question 58

You are on a motorway. When can you use hazard warning lights?

Mark two answers

- a. When a vehicle is following too closely
- b. When you slow down quickly because of danger ahead
- c. When you are towing another vehicle
- d. When driving on the hard shoulder
- e. When you have broken down on the hard shoulder

Question 59

You are on a motorway. The car in front switches on its hazard warning lights whilst moving. This means

Mark one answer

ⓐ they are going to take the next exit
ⓑ there is a danger ahead
ⓒ there is a police car in the left lane
ⓓ they are trying to change lanes

Answers and explanations

Q001   d,e,f
Q002   a
Q003   b,c,d,e
Q004   b Warning other traffic first helps stop the accident getting even worse.
Q005   a,b,e
Q006   a
Q007   a,c,f
    Injuries should be dealt with in the order Airway, Breathing then Circulation and bleeding.
Q008   a
Q009   a,b,d
Q010   a,c,e
    Note that these are the things to which you should give urgent priority.
Q011   d,e,f
Q012   a,b,e
    You should not move injured people unless they are in danger; nor should you give them anything to drink.
Q013   a,c,f
Q014   a,e
Q015   a,c,d,e
Q016   c
Q017   b,c
Q018   c,d,e
Q019   a

Answers and explanations

Q020 b Note that this is the FIRST
      thing to do. By warning other
      traffic you help reduce the risk
      of more collisions.

Q021 b

Q022 b,d,e

Q023 b

Q024 c

Q025 d

Q026 c,d

Q027 d

Q028 c

Q029 c

Q030 b If you move the casualty you
      may worsen their injury.

Q031 d

Q032 b

Q033 d

Q034 a,b

Q035 b,c,d

Q036 a

Q037 c 45 metres is recommended
      on two-way roads and 150
      metres on motorways and
      dual carriageways.

Q038 b

Q039 b

Q040 c

Q041 b,d,e

Q042 a,b,c,e

Q043 c This usually means another
      train is coming.

Q044 a,b,d

Q045 a A train may arrive within
      seconds so 'a' is the only
      safe possibility.

Q046 a Your first action is to get
      everyone to safety.

Q047 c,d
      You will need both hands
      firmly on the wheel in order
      to control the car, and using
      the gears or brakes is likely to
      make your car swerve. When
      possible, it is safest just to let
      your car roll to a halt at the
      side of the road.

Q048 c,e

Q049 c The hard shoulder of a
      motorway is a dangerous
      place and 'c' is the safest
      course of action. It can be
      particularly dangerous to try
      to change an offside wheel
      as you may be very close to
      fast-moving traffic in the
      left-hand lane.

Q050 a The engine cut-out switch
      stops the engine and shuts
      off all electrical circuits,
      thus reducing the risk of fire
      in an accident.

Answers and explanations

Q051   a

Q052   b

Q053   b,e

Q054   a,d,e

Q055   a

Q056   c It would be extremely dangerous to try and retrieve the bag yourself.

Q057   a

Q058   b,e

Q059   b

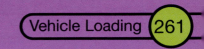

Driving Theory
Test
Questions

2000/2001

Vehicle Loading

BSM
We won't fail you

Question 1

Overloading your vehicle can seriously affect the

Mark two answers

- ⓐ gearbox
- ⓑ steering
- ⓒ handling
- ⓓ battery life
- ⓔ journey time

Question 2

Who is responsible for making sure that a vehicle is not overloaded?

Mark one answer

- ⓐ The driver or rider of the vehicle
- ⓑ The owner of the items being carried
- ⓒ The person who loaded the vehicle
- ⓓ The owner of the vehicle

Question 3

On which TWO occasions might you inflate your tyres to more than the recommended normal pressure?

Mark two answers

- ⓐ When the roads are slippery
- ⓑ When driving fast for a long distance
- ⓒ When the tyre tread is worn below 2mm
- ⓓ When carrying a heavy load
- ⓔ When the weather is cold
- ⓕ When the vehicle is fitted with anti-lock brakes

Question 4

Any load that is carried on a luggage rack MUST be

Mark one answer

- ⓐ securely fastened when riding
- ⓑ carried only when strictly necessary
- ⓒ visible when you are riding
- ⓓ covered with plastic sheeting

Question 5

Any load that is carried on a roof rack MUST be

Mark one answer

- ⓐ securely fastened when driving
- ⓑ carried only when strictly necessary
- ⓒ as light as possible
- ⓓ covered with plastic sheeting

Question 6

A heavy load on your roof rack will

Mark one answer

- ⓐ improve the road holding
- ⓑ reduce the stopping distance
- ⓒ make the steering lighter
- ⓓ reduce stability

Question 7

Which THREE are suitable restraints for a child under three years?

Mark three answers

- a. A child seat
- b. An adult holding a child
- c. An adult seat belt
- d. A lap belt
- e. A harness
- f. A baby carrier

Question 8

What do child locks in a vehicle do?

Mark one answer

- a. Lock the seat belt buckles in place
- b. Lock the rear windows in the up position
- c. Stop children from opening rear doors
- d. Stop the rear seats from tipping forward

Question 9

Your vehicle is fitted with child safety door locks. You should use these so that children inside the car cannot open

Mark one answer

- a. the right-hand doors
- b. the left-hand doors
- c. the rear doors
- d. any of the doors

Question 10

You want to tow a trailer with your motorcycle. Which one applies?

Mark one answer

- a. The motorcycle should be attached to a sidecar
- b. The trailer should weigh more than the motorcycle
- c. The trailer should be fitted with brakes
- d. The trailer should not be more than 1 metre (3 feet 3 inches) wide

Question 11

You are planning to tow a caravan. Which of these will mostly help to aid the vehicle handling?

Mark one answer

- a. A jockey-wheel fitted to the towbar
- b. Power steering fitted to the towing vehicle
- c. Anti-lock brakes fitted to the towing vehicle
- d. A stabiliser fitted to the towbar

Question 12

A trailer must stay securely hitched-up to the towing vehicle. What additional safety device can be fitted to the trailer braking system?

Mark one answer

- a. Stabiliser
- b. Jockey wheel
- c. Corner steadies
- d. Breakaway cable

Question 13

If a trailer swerves or snakes when you are towing it you should

Mark one answer

ⓐ ease off the accelerator and reduce your speed

ⓑ let go of the steering wheel and let it correct itself

ⓒ brake hard and hold the pedal down

ⓓ increase your speed as quickly as possible

Question 14

Are passengers allowed to ride in a caravan that is being towed?

Mark one answer

ⓐ Yes, if they are over fourteen

ⓑ No, not at any time

ⓒ Only if all the seats in the towing vehicle are full

ⓓ Only if a stabiliser is fitted

Question 15

You are towing a caravan along a motorway. The caravan begins to swerve from side to side. What should you do?

Mark one answer

ⓐ Ease off the accelerator slowly

ⓑ Steer sharply from side to side

ⓒ Do an emergency stop

ⓓ Speed up very quickly

Question 16

If a trailer swerves or snakes when you are towing it you should

Mark one answer

ⓐ ease off the throttle and reduce your speed

ⓑ let go of the handlebars and let it correct itself

ⓒ brake hard and hold the brake on

ⓓ increase your speed as quickly as possible

Question 17

How can you stop a caravan snaking from side to side?

Mark one answer

ⓐ Turn the steering wheel slowly to each side

ⓑ Accelerate to increase your speed

ⓒ Stop as quickly as you can

ⓓ Slow down very gradually

Question 18

You are towing a small trailer on a busy three-lane motorway. All the lanes are open. You must

Mark two answers

ⓐ not exceed 60 mph

ⓑ not overtake

ⓒ have a stabiliser fitted

ⓓ use only the left and centre lanes

Question 19

You have a side-car fitted to your motorcycle. What effect will it have?

Mark one answer

- a Reduce stability
- b Make steering lighter
- c Increase stopping distance
- d Increase fuel economy

Question 20

When riding with a sidecar attached for the first time you should

Mark two answers

- a keep your speed down
- b be able to stop more quickly
- c accelerate quickly round bends
- d approach corners more carefully

Question 21

A trailer on a motorcycle must be no wider than

Mark one answer

- a 1 metre (3 feet 3 inches)
- b 1/2 metre (1 foot 8 inches)
- c 1 1/2 metres (4 feet 11 inches)
- d 2 metres (6 feet 6 inches)

Question 22

Before fitting a side-car, riders should

Mark one answer

- a have the wheels of their bike balanced
- b have their bike's engine tuned
- c pass the extended bike test
- d check that their bike is suitable

Question 23

You want to tow a trailer behind your motorcycle. You should

Mark two answers

- a display a 'long vehicle' sign
- b fit a larger battery
- c have a full motorcycle licence
- d ensure that your engine is more than 125cc
- e ensure that your machine has shaft drive

Question 24

When may a learner motorcyclist carry a pillion passenger?

Mark one answer

- a If the passenger holds a full licence
- b Not at any time
- c If the rider is undergoing training
- d If the passenger is over 21

Question 25

Which THREE must a learner motorcyclist under 21 NOT do?

Mark three answers

- a Ride a motorcycle with an engine capacity greater than 125cc
- b Pull a trailer
- c Carry a pillion passenger
- d Ride faster than 30 mph
- e Use the right-hand lane on dual carriageways

Question 26

Pillion passengers should

Mark one answer

ⓐ have a provisional motorcycle licence

ⓑ be lighter than the rider

ⓒ always wear a helmet

ⓓ signal for the rider

Question 27

Pillion passengers should

Mark one answer

ⓐ give the rider directions

ⓑ lean with the rider when going round bends

ⓒ check the road behind for the rider

ⓓ give arm signals for the rider

Question 28

When carrying extra weight on a motorcycle, you may need to make adjustments to the

Mark three answers

ⓐ headlight

ⓑ gears

ⓒ suspension

ⓓ tyres

ⓔ footrests

Question 29

To carry a pillion passenger your bike should be fitted with

Mark two answers

ⓐ rear footrests

ⓑ an engine of 250cc or over

ⓒ a top box

ⓓ a grab handle

ⓔ a proper passenger seat

Question 30

To obtain the full category 'A' licence through the accelerated or direct access scheme, your motorcycle must be

Mark one answer

ⓐ solo with maximum power 25kw (33 bhp)

ⓑ solo with maximum power of 11kw(14.6 bhp)

ⓒ fitted with a sidecar and have minimum power of 35kw (46.6 bhp)

ⓓ solo with minimum power of 35 kw (46.6 bhp)

Question 31

When you are going around a corner your pillion passenger should

Mark one answer

ⓐ give arm signals for you

ⓑ check behind for other vehicles

ⓒ lean with you on bends

ⓓ lean to one side to see ahead

Question 32

Which of these may need to be adjusted when carrying a pillion passenger?

Mark one answer

- ⓐ Indicators
- ⓑ Exhaust
- ⓒ Fairing
- ⓓ Headlight

Question 33

Your motorcycle is fitted with a top box. It is unwise to carry a heavy load in the top box because it may

Mark three answers

- ⓐ reduce stability
- ⓑ improve stability
- ⓒ make turning easier
- ⓓ cause high-speed weave
- ⓔ cause low-speed wobble
- ⓕ increase fuel economy

Question 34

You are towing a trailer with your motorcycle. You should remember that your

Mark one answer

- ⓐ stopping distance may increase
- ⓑ fuel consumption will improve
- ⓒ tyre grip will increase
- ⓓ stability will improve

Answers and explanations

Q001 b,c

Q002 a

Q003 b,d

Q004 a

Q005 a The word 'MUST' in the question makes 'a' correct.

Q006 d A heavy load on the roof will shift the centre of gravity of your vehicle and could make you more likely to skid or roll over.

Q007 a,e,f

Q008 c Child locks prevent the rear doors being opened from the inside.

Q009 c

Q010 d The laden weight of the trailer must not exceed 150kg or two-thirds of the kerbside weight of the motorcycle, whichever is less.

Q011 d

Q012 d

Q013 a Options 'b', 'c' or 'd' would all be likely to make the problem worse.

Q014 b

Q015 a

Q016 a

Q017 d

Q018 a,d

Q019   c   The side-car is extra weight and is likely to increase your overall stopping distance.

Q020   a,d

You will need to adapt your riding technique when riding a bike with a side-car, particularly on bends and when turning. The side-car must be steered because you cannot lean the machine over.

Q021   a

Q022   d

Q023   c,d

Q024   b

Q025   a,b,c

Q026   c

Q027   b

Q028   a,c,d

Q029   a,e

Q030   d

Q031   c

Q032   d

Q033   a,d,e

Q034   a

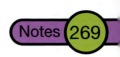

Notes

For information on learning to drive with a BSM instructor please contact your local BSM centre on:

08457 276 276

BSM instructors operate under a franchise with
The British School of Motoring Limited, the largest organisation of its kind
in the world.

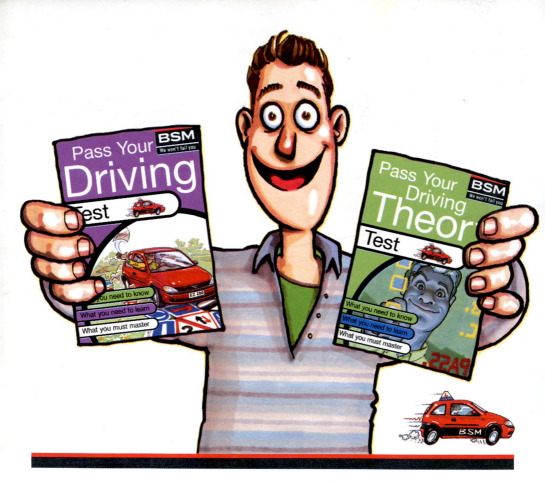

The two additional books in the series, *Pass Your Driving Test* and *Pass Your Driving Theory Test*, are available from all BSM centres and from all good bookshops.